The Guide to Oklahoma Wildflowers

THE GUIDE TO
Oklahoma Wildflowers

by Patricia Folley

University of Iowa Press, Iowa City

A BUR OAK GUIDE
Holly Carver, series editor

With deepest respect, this book is dedicated to Jim Estes, who gave me the keys to the flora of Oklahoma and to the herbarium at the University of Oklahoma.

University of Iowa Press
Iowa City 52242
Copyright © 2011 by the
University of Iowa Press
www.uiowapress.org
PRINTED IN CHINA

Design by Kristina Kachele Design, llc

No part of this book may be reproduced or used in any form or by any means without permission in writing from the publisher. All reasonable steps have been taken to contact copyright holders of material used in this book. The publisher would be pleased to make suitable arrangements with any whom it has not been possible to reach.

Unless stated otherwise, all photos were taken by the author.

The University of Iowa Press is a member of Green Press Initiative and is committed to preserving natural resources.

Printed on acid-free paper

Library of Congress Cataloging-in-Publication Data
Folley, Patricia.
The guide to Oklahoma wildflowers /
by Patricia Folley.—1st ed.
p.   cm.—(A Bur Oak guide)
Includes bibliographical references and index.
ISBN-13: 978-1-60938-046-5 (pbk.)
ISBN-10: 1-60938-046-0 (pbk.)
ISBN-13: 978-1-60938-047-2 (e-book)
ISBN-10: 1-60938-047-9 (e-book)
1. Wild flowers—Oklahoma—Identification.
2. Wild flowers—Oklahoma—Pictorial works.
I. Title.   II. Series: Bur Oak guide.
QK181.F65 2012
582.13'09766—dc22   2011014154

Contents

Preface and Acknowledgments ⟩ vii
How to Use This Book ⟩ xi
A Word about Collecting ⟩ xv
Oklahoma Wildflower Families ⟩ 1
Oklahoma Wildflowers ⟩ 17
Glossary ⟩ 217
Bibliography ⟩ 219
Name Index ⟩ 221
Color Index ⟩ 229

Preface and Acknowledgments

This book is for you if you are a newcomer to Oklahoma, a gardener, a Scout or 4-H or Campfire leader, a schoolteacher, or a parent. In it, you will find pictures of Oklahoma wildflowers growing where nature put them, along roadsides, in parks and fields, and in your own backyard.

I was a child of ten when my family moved into a house on the edge of Oklahoma City. Already an ardent reader, I was surprised to find that the few books in the library with any pictures at all didn't show the flowers in my neighborhood. How can you describe a flower to someone when you don't have a name for it? I drew pictures of flowers, tried dipping them in melted wax (disgusting), and finally just gave up and gave them names of my own. Anyone who has ever named a plant "fairy princess powder puffs" will recognize sensitive briar (*Mimosa nuttallii*) when she sees it again.

Years later, when Doyle McCoy began assembling his roadside guides to Oklahoma plants, I began to get an inkling of the accepted naming system. This system, begun by Carl Linnaeus in the 1800s, provides a structure for understanding the different kinds of plants. Oklahoma's some 2,500 species of plants are first placed in some 173 families, which are further divided into some 850 genera (the first part of the binomial scientific name). Those divisions represent the relatedness of individual species. For example, Oklahoma's fifteen or so species of sunflowers are all first-named to the genus *Helianthus*, each then getting a species name such as *maximiliani*, which securely identifies Maximilian's sunflower as *Helianthus maximiliani*. Scientific names are currently undergoing significant revision as DNA research progresses. In this book I have used the most currently accepted names available to the *Flora of Oklahoma*. Most of the common names come from Taylor and Taylor's *Annotated List* (see Bibliography).

Some thirty years ago, when we moved to the wild acreage where I now live, I started trying to name every plant I found here. Some were covered by McCoy's roadside guides, but more were not, so I enrolled in classes at the University of Oklahoma to learn more. By the time I retired, I knew enough to become a volunteer at the University of Oklahoma's herbarium, where I still enjoy my one day a week of playing botanist. Dr. McCoy has died, and his little roadside guides are out of print and out of date. Thus, this book.

I took all the photographs (except those shown on pages 46, 49, and 77) using a Pentax camera equipped with a 1:1 macro lens and slide film. I have shown them all over Oklahoma in the popular slide programs I have taken to garden centers, Oklahoma Native Plant Society meetings, and schools—wherever I could get an audience. Perhaps someone who has this book will become the next volunteer who will bring PowerPoint shows to eager audiences. Botany is a wonderful hobby, and who knows where it will lead you.

This book is a selection from the many slide programs I have offered. I wanted everyone to know about the wildflowers. But as I am an amateur without a degree in botany, along the way there were many real botanists who offered help, guidance, and suggestions.

Foremost among those who contributed was James Estes, who arranged my position as volunteer herbarium assistant at the University of Oklahoma's Bebb Herbarium. Once there, Curator Emeritus George Goodman and graduate student Staria Vanderpool willingly and kindly offered help until I was able to work on my own.

Election to the editorial committee of the *Flora of Oklahoma* project was my introduction to the scientific description of flowering plants. Committee members who were most helpful included Chief Editor Ronald Tyrl, Susan Barber, Paul Buck, Wayne Elisens, Larry Magrath, and Connie Taylor, all professors of botany at Oklahoma universities.

Access to the wildlands of Oklahoma was provided by Nora Jones and Jim Erwin of The Nature Conservancy. Those explorations into wild swamps, stony prairies, and marshy wetlands were the occasion of many of the photographs in this book.

Audiences and field companions came from the Oklahoma Native Plant Society and the Oklahoma Academy of Science. Jim Norman provided priceless access to the orchid sites of eastern Oklahoma. Forrest Johnson, of the Oklahoma Biological Survey, was my partner in the botanical exploration and documentation of The Nature Conservancy's Pontotoc Ridge Preserve.

How to Use This Book

When I started compiling the photographs for this book, I was simultaneously working with the Oklahoma Native Plant Society, the University of Oklahoma's Bebb Herbarium, The Nature Conservancy's Oklahoma chapter, the Oklahoma State Fair as judge of the 4-H wildflower exhibits, and the *Flora of Oklahoma* project.

There was an obvious need for a place for people interested in wildflowers but not able to study them scientifically to go for immediate help. So, this book is organized in a way that will allow a child of ten or a gardener of a certain age or a traveler passing through to identify at a glance the plant before her. Most of the selections are of wildflowers that are accessible along roadsides and in parks throughout the state. A few are rare and hard to find, but it is worth a considerable effort to find them. Using the Color Index will help you find out whether the plant you see is the one you want to know about. The index is divided into four color groups: white, cream, green, brown, straw; red, orange, yellow; pink, orchid, purple, rose, magenta, rose-pink; and blue, violet, blue-violet, lavender. For example, the bloom of great bulrush is first green; the pollinated flower turns brown. Thus in the index, great bulrush is under the category white, cream, green, brown, straw, listed as green and brown; hoary vervain, with its deep blue or purple flowers, is under the categories blue, violet, blue-violet, lavender and pink, orchid, purple, rose, magenta, rose-pink.

Each described species has two or more photographs, one showing the entire plant growing in its natural habitat and another, a close-up view, showing the plant in bloom. Where I could not avoid using technical terms, a definition is included in the text (or the Glossary).

For more help in finding a name for the plant you have blooming before you, the map shows the diversity of Oklahoma habitats, roughly divided north-south by I-40 and east-west by I-35, as well as the Cross Timbers, an area originally dominated by post oaks and blackjack oaks, that separates the more heavily forested eastern United States from the almost treeless Great Plains. Each area has its own, if relatively small, mountains. The northeast has the Ozarks, shading to the Great Plains toward the west. The southeast starts with the Ouachitas and terminates with the Red River floodplain. Southwest, there are the Arbuckles and the Wichitas, with the canyons of the branches of the Red River beyond. And even the northwest is not a flat prairie; following the various forks of the Canadian, Cimarron, and Arkansas Rivers are sand dunes and the strange, low Glass Mountains. The Panhandle, way out west, is a shortgrass prairie habitat of its own, terminating in the beginning of Rocky Mountain flora at Black Mesa.

Comprehending families and their relationships is essential to comprehending the overall organization of a flora. Thus I have included not just representative wildflowers but a representative range of families to introduce the structure of Oklahoma's plant communities. The book begins with descriptions of all the families included, followed by the wildflower species themselves, presented in taxonomic sequence organized by family, implying that there is a relationship between those shown and those near

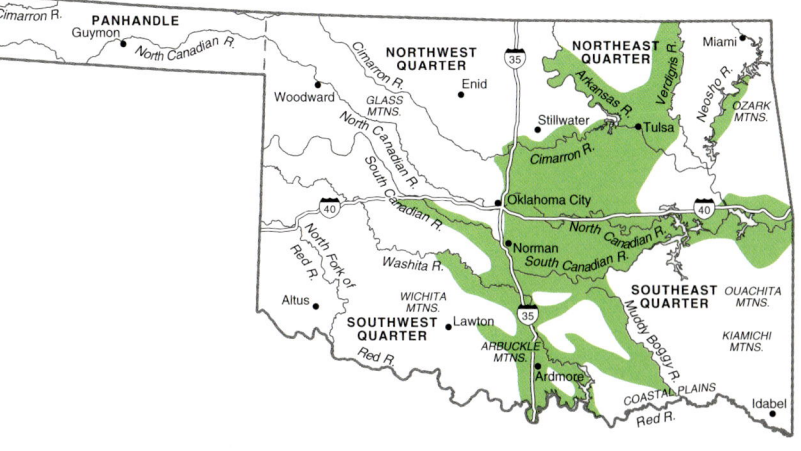

Oklahoma's geographic sections, with the Cross Timbers shown in green.

matches that might be confronted. Often a plant's close relatives will be those nearest to it in the book. A determined Scout or gardener can then go to my bibliography, to bookstores, and to libraries to learn more about the related plants.

All of the photographs are of living plants in the places where they grow naturally. I have been scrupulous about not collecting specimens from the plants I used as models. As you continue to grow in the fascinating hobby of wildflower appreciation, you too can spread the concept of wildflower conservation. Even experts cannot know the true value of any living species to its habitat. Before you collect, consider whether the living population can spare even one.

Conservation starts with knowing what is there. Someone who sees only "weeds" will not be motivated to go far to protect them. In the developed world, a patch of grass that can still produce blue-eyed grass, a pond that supports lotus, or a wetland of any description is worth watching, learning about, and growing to love.

A Word about Collecting

There are, in the simplest terms, three kinds of plant collectors: botanists who make collections for plant research collections, called herbaria; gardeners who bring home interesting wild plants for their own satisfaction; and commercial collectors, who dig wild plants for resale.

I am one of the first kind, as I collect Oklahoma plants, carefully and responsibly, for the Bebb Herbarium at the University of Oklahoma. If the population is large, I may collect extra plants for the herbaria maintained at Oklahoma State University and other institutions. We make these collections to preserve a historical record of the plant's presence at a time and place, which is written on a label that is pasted to the mounting sheet. These recorded plant specimens are deposited in environmentally controlled, protected, pest-free facilities for perpetuity; they are available for researchers who need to study them. We are lucky to have in Oklahoma some of the plants collected by early explorers of Indian Territory.

Possibly you who are reading this book are, or will become, the second kind of collector. You like plants, enjoy learning about them, and want to have them growing around your own home. There are some things you need to know before collecting.

First, while no plants in Oklahoma are on the endangered species list, and federal law permits collecting all of them, there are certainly quite a few that have become very rare and should not be collected. You can recognize a rare plant when you find only one or two in a location and have not seen any others on the way there, or if the location itself is rare—a bog, for example. I will tell you about one such place (but I will not tell you where it is!).

A small group of us had been driving for about an hour through the countryside without seeing a town. After crossing a little bridge, we found ourselves on a gravel road that wound through gentle hills until we didn't even know in what direction we were heading. Finally we stopped at a rocky hillside and pushed through brush for about a hundred yards, to a shady spring where lady's slippers grew on a bank that was about ten feet long. Nearly twenty of them were in bloom, but we knew we were in a sacred place, took pictures, sighed, and went on.

On the other hand, if you want to try growing a soft sunflower (*Helianthus mollis*) and have found the plant abundant along a country road, you need only ask the property owner's permission to dig a few. It will not be worth your trouble digging them, though, unless you also know how to keep them alive at your home. So, look at the kind of soil, whether sand or clay or dark loam or rocks, and the amount of moisture available to the plant. Then consider how much sunlight it needs. On the whole, wild plants are remarkable survivors when their ecological needs are met. Some thrive so well in gardens—trumpet creeper, for example—that you will wish you had never moved them.

Many of the wildflowers found growing along state highways have been planted by the Beautification Department of the Oklahoma Department of Transportation. The department cannot give you permission to dig those, as they are public property. Since the ODOT buys all its seed from commercial suppliers, you can do the same and have legal plants of your own. Or you might collect a small amount of seed to try in your own habitat, and start a colony of your own. Planting from seed is always preferable.

And if you are the third kind of collector, ripping up wild places to provide a little extra cash, my advice is this: Get a job! Oklahoma has had enough habitat destruction in the name of dam building, farming, lumbering, and development to render every remaining wild place a thing to cherish.

Want to learn more about Oklahoma wild plants, meet people who share your interests, and find out about field trips to some great places? Contact the Oklahoma Native Plant Society, c/o Tulsa Garden Center, 2435 S. Peoria, Tulsa OK 74114. The website is www.usao.edu/~onps/.

Oklahoma Wildflower Families

Alismataceae, water plantain family

Oklahoma has 14 species in 3 genera of water plantains, well named because all are found in water or mud. They are plants with milky sap and often showy, 3-petaled white flowers. All surfaces are smooth, and the fruits are simple achenes (small, hard fruits with a single seed). See page 17.

Poaceae, grass family

The grasses are the second-largest family in Oklahoma in terms of species and, by observation, the most numerous in terms of individual plants. Animals, including humans, use grasses for food more so than all other kinds of plants. Oklahoma has 308 species of grasses in 91 genera. This guide includes a few grasses that every Oklahoman should know. Luckily, they are ones you can identify at sight, without special training or equipment.

To decide whether your plant is a grass or not, look for leaves that wrap around the round stems for a short distance before folding out into the light, and for a joint or node between each leaf and the next. Grass flowers usually have 2 to 4 little bracts—specialized leaves directly under the flower—below the stamens and pistils and no petals. See pages 18–23.

Cyperaceae, sedge family

The old saying "grasses are round, but sedges have edges" is generally true of those slender stems, but there are exceptions. For example, *Eleocharis* is a genus of sedges whose stems may be flat, round, fluted, octagonal, and even triangular in cross section. Sedges have grasslike flowers with only 1 specialized scale under the flower parts. Like grasses, they have 1 seed per flower. Oklahoma has about 150 species of sedges in 15 genera. Although sedges tend not to become agricultural commodities, they perform an important service. Because they grow preferentially on wet or very wet soils, the stems and roots form a tight mat that holds the soil against erosion. Birds and small mammals eat the small seeds of sedges. See pages 24–27.

Araceae, arum family

Oklahoma has 4 species in 3 genera of the arum family. They are notable for their club-shaped flower spike, called a spadix, that is the "Jack" in the "pulpit" formed by the floral bract. See page 28.

Xyridaceae, yelloweyed grass family

There are only 2 species of these pretty little bog plants in Oklahoma. The family is primarily tropical. The flowers are produced on small brownish conelike structures. See page 29.

Commelinaceae, dayflower family

Oklahoma has 12 species in 2 genera. Many adapt easily to garden culture and are worth collecting. The sap is mucilaginous; children sometimes call them snotweeds. The flowers have 6 stamens, 3 green sepals, and 3 colored petals, 1 of which may be white and tiny. The flowers wither after 1 day's exposure, but there are more to come. The fruits are capsules—dry and papery, with dry seeds inside. See pages 30–31.

Pontederiaceae, pickerelweed family

Pickerelweeds are plants of muddy shorelines and shallow water. We have 4 species in 2 genera in Oklahoma. The fruits are capsules—dry and papery, with dry seeds inside— or single seeds. The dense fibrous roots make a natural nursery for tiny hatchling fish. See page 32.

Juncaceae, rush family

These plants are very similar to grasses and sedges overall, but their stiff, light brown flowers are more like those of a lily, though much smaller. The fruits are capsules, dry and papery, with many tiny dry seeds inside. See pages 33–34.

Liliaceae, lily family

Currently, the lily family is considered to include all the species of the amaryllis family, too, so that Oklahoma has 40 species in 22 genera. They are among the best-loved and most attractive of our wildflowers. The flowers usually have 6 "tepals"—either petals or sepals, or both—in 2 whorls of 3 each, and they also have 6 stamens. The fruits are either capsules or berries. See pages 35–42.

Iridaceae, iris family

Oklahoma has 11 species of iris relatives in 5 genera. Iris plants are known for their linear leaves creased along the midrib, with each lower leaf clasping the next in that fold. Like lilies, they have 6 "tepals"—both petal and sepal—in 2 whorls, but they have 3 stamens where lilies have 6, and the stigmas are joined with the petals into a tube. Their fruits are dry and papery capsules with many dry seeds. See pages 43–45.

Orchidaceae, orchid family

Oklahoma has 33 species of orchids in 18 genera. All of ours are terrestrial and some are really beautiful, but they are very particular about habitat and so should not be transplanted into habitats that may be more comfortable to people. While some occur in widespread locations, all should be considered rare. See pages 46–51.

Polygonaceae, buckwheat family

This large family of herbs is well represented in Oklahoma, with 38 species in 5 genera. Many are quite common. Most have swollen joints at the nodes that bear a band of loose, sometimes fringed tissue around those joints. See pages 52–54.

Nyctaginaceae, four o'clock family

Oklahoma has 10 species of four o'clocks in 4 genera. These flowers lack petals, but some have colorful sepals. The familiar garden four o'clock, a native of Mexico, sometimes persists for a while out of gardens. The fruits are fairly large dry seeds, somewhat top-shaped. See page 55.

Portulacaceae, purslane family

Oklahoma's 9 species in 3 genera are all small herbs, several of them pretty enough for gardens. They have succulent leaves, and the fruits are small, dry capsules with dry seeds inside. See pages 56–57.

Caryophyllaceae, pink family

Oklahoma has 32 species in 15 genera of this large family. They are herbs with 5-petaled flowers, which usually have a notch in the petal tip. The fruit is usually a capsule (dry and papery) bearing many small dry seeds. See pages 58–61.

Nelumbonaceae, lotus family

This is the only member of the lotus family that is native to Oklahoma. Lotus plants may be found in the quiet, still waters of ponds and lakes; they have large round leaves that float on the surface. The dried seed heads of lotus are staples of the florist industry. See page 62.

Ranunculaceae, buttercup family

Oklahoma has 37 species of buttercups in 10 genera. They are surely the most wildly variable family in the state, with growth forms including woody vines, prairie herbs, and water-floaters. Some have sepals that look like petals, some have no petals at all, and the petals vary from single to the contorted ones of columbine. See pages 63–69.

Papaveraceae, poppy family

Oklahoma has 6 species of poppy in 4 genera. All of these plants have thick, opaque sap. Several species of Eurasian garden poppies may also be found along roadsides and in old fields where they have escaped cultivation. See pages 70–71.

Fumariaceae, fumitory family

Six species in 2 genera make up Oklahoma's wealth of fumitories. One species or another may be found in any part of the state. All the *Corydalis* species may be called by the common name scrambled eggs. The fruits are dry and papery capsules, with dry seeds inside. See pages 72–74.

Brassicaceae, mustard family

Oklahoma has 69 species of mustards in 30 genera. Many are small and weedy, with small flowers, but there are some truly beautiful plants in this family, too. The fruits are dry, papery capsules, mostly long and thin. See pages 75–81.

Capparaceae, caper family

Oklahoma has 7 species in 3 genera of these strong-scented herbs. The plants are usually sticky-hairy, with 3- or 5-parted leaves and 4-petaled flowers with the stamens waving far out from the center. The fruits are dry, papery capsules with dry seeds inside. See pages 82–83.

Crassulaceae, stonecrop family

Oklahoma has only 3 species in this interesting family, all small herbs. They usually have succulent leaves and fruits that are dry capsules, and they favor dry, exposed sites that allow few competitors to thrive. See pages 84–85.

Rosaceae, rose family

With 67 species in 19 genera, Oklahoma is well endowed with roses. Many of them are trees, such as plums, pears, and hawthorns, and a good many more are shrubs, such as blackberries and mountain mahogany. All are distinguished by having 5 clearly separate petals and many anthers. Their fruits are berries, aggregates (like blackberries), pomes (like apples), or even small dry achenes (small, hard fruits with a single seed). See pages 86–90.

Fabaceae, bean or legume family

One of our largest families, its 53 genera and 178 species are grouped into 3 subfamilies—Mimosa, Caesalpinia, and Fabaceae—based on the shapes of leaves and flowers. The most common flower type resembles a sunbonnet or butterfly; others look more like powderpuffs because of their long stamens. The fruits are beanlike with one to several seeds borne in pods. As a family, these are very important food plants for humans on all continents. See pages 91–115.

Krameriaceae, ratany family

Long considered part of the pea family, this little ground-hugger is now the sole representative of its family in Oklahoma. The ratany family is an American family comprising only 25 species. It ranges from Chile in South America to the southern United States. There are 4 species, mostly shrubs, in Texas. See page 116.

Geraniaceae, geranium family

Eight species of geranium are found in Oklahoma, only half of them native. All are small herbs with 5 petals and with the styles formed into "beaks" on the small dry seeds. See pages 117–118.

Oxalidaceae, wood sorrel family

Five species make up this small family in Oklahoma. Four of them are native. They all contain oxalic acid, which gives a pleasant pickle taste to the leaves. All have 5 petals, and the fruits are capsules. See pages 119–120.

Linaceae, linen family, flax family

There are 8 species of flax in Oklahoma, all in the genus *Linum*. The European herb *Linum usitatissimum* is the source of the flax fiber from which linen cloth is produced and may sometimes be found growing wild in Oklahoma. *Linum* petals are very easily detached, usually falling when picked. The fruits are capsules. See pages 121–123.

Polygalaceae, milkwort family

With just 7 species, all in the genus *Polygala*, this family of small herbs would seem insignificant except that they are all pretty in a dainty sort of manner. The name comes from their historical use in stimulating milk flow in new mothers. They have intricate, irregular flowers. The fruits are 2-seeded capsules. See pages 124–125.

Euphorbiaceae, spurge family

With 51 species in 11 genera, this is one of the more populous plant families in Oklahoma. Most of them are interesting chemically if not artistically: they have milky sap that is often poisonous, sometimes medicinal, and usually bad-tasting. A hand lens is best to appreciate the often tiny flowers. The fruits are 3-celled capsules (dry and papery) with 1 or 2 dry seeds in each cell. See pages 126–130.

Malvaceae, mallow family

There are 22 species in 10 genera of Oklahoma mallows. A few are among the most common and best-loved of our wildflowers. Mallows share the habit of carrying the stamens closely around the pistil, making a little "pom-pom on a stick" formation that is familiar to anyone who has ever grown cotton or okra, two other members of this family. They make a 5- or 10-parted capsule-like fruit that splits to dispense the seeds. See pages 131–132.

Hypericaceae, St. John's-wort family

There are 15 species of St. John's-wort in Oklahoma in 2 genera. All of the *Hypericum* species have yellow flowers, with 4 petals in a cross-like arrangement, and a showy tuft of silky stamens. All are erect herbs or small shrubby plants with opposite leaves. See pages 133–134.

Violaceae, violet family

Oklahoma has 17 species of violets in 2 genera. Ours are all small plants with 5-petaled flowers that are irregularly shaped. The fruits are dry, papery capsules bearing many small seeds, each of which has an ant-attracting attachment to enhance distribution. See pages 135–138.

Passifloraceae, passion flower family

Oklahoma's 2 species of passion flowers are vines and have the easily identifiable passion flower blooms. Otherwise they are as different as they can be within that description. The fruits are berries that look more like gourds. See page 139.

Loasaceae, stickleaf family

The stickleafs get their name from the incredibly clingy leaf hairs, which can outlast several washings of the garment to which they have pressed themselves. These hairs are beautiful under a low-power microscope. Oklahoma has 7 species in 2 genera. They have 5 to many petals, and the fruits are capsules. See pages 140–141.

Cactaceae, cactus family

Oklahoma's share of the cactus family amounts to 16 species in 7 genera. The distribution may be larger than those shown, for the information is based on specimens deposited in herbaria, and cacti are notably difficult to gather and press. Some have big, beautiful flowers with many petals and fruits that are fleshy or dry. See pages 142–145.

Lythraceae, loosestrife family

Oklahoma has 7 species of true loosestrife in 5 water-loving genera. The leaves are usually opposite, positioned 2 to a node along a stem, and the stems are square. When they have petals, there are 6, and the fruits are dry and papery capsules, with dry seeds inside. See page 146.

Melastomaceae, meadow-beauty family

This large tropical family, centered in Brazil, shares only 2 species with Oklahoma, but they are real treasures. Most other members of the Melastomaceae family are shrubs or small trees. See page 147.

Onagraceae, evening primrose family

Oklahoma enjoys a wealth of beautiful wildflowers in the Onagraceae, with 7 genera and 43 species. These are usually yellow, white, or pink to rose in color and often are night bloomers. As a rule, there are 4 separate petals, and the fruits are dry, papery capsules. See pages 148–152.

Apiaceae, carrot family

There are 56 species in 35 genera of carrot family plants growing wild in Oklahoma, and they are found in all areas. The umbrella-shaped flower heads with many small 5-petaled flowers, usually yellow or white, and leaves that clasp hollow stems and are often pungent or fragrant are characteristic. Many of the Apiaceae are useful as food or seasonings or medicines. Others are poisonous, including some of the more common ones. See pages 153–159.

Primulaceae, primrose family

With only 12 species in 7 genera of this interesting family in Oklahoma, you'll have to look hard to find more than the spectacular shooting-star. Most of them are small and inconspicuous. See page 160.

Loganiaceae, Indian pink family, logania family

Oklahoma has only 4 species in this mostly tropical family, and they are about as different from each other as it is possible to be. They have in common opposite, simple leaves with smooth margins, tubular flowers, and a tendency to contain poisons such as strychnine. See page 161.

Gentianaceae, gentian family

Oklahoma's 11 species of gentian relatives in 6 genera are neither as showy nor as common as they are further north, but they are well worth knowing. They have 4 or 5 petals, and the fruits are dry, papery capsules. See pages 162–164.

Apocynaceae, dogbane or milkweed family

The family's defining characteristics are its milky sap and modified flower parts followed by pods that may be long and slender or plump and pealike, filled with many seeds and long, silky hairs. See pages 165–171.

Convolvulaceae, morning glory family

With 17 species in 7 genera in Oklahoma, at least 1 of these often pretty plants should be in every neighborhood. Morning glories are mostly vines, more or less twining without tendrils, with the flaring bell shape characteristic of morning glories. They bear seeds in dry, papery capsules. See pages 172–174.

Polemoniaceae, phlox family

Oklahoma's 12 species in 3 genera of phloxes are herbs with showy, tubular flowers that flare outward, trumpet-like. The seeds are borne in dry, papery capsules. As they are often dug to plant in flower beds, they may sometimes be found outside their natural habitats, but they are notoriously difficult to sustain. See pages 175–177.

Hydrophyllaceae, waterleaf family

Oklahoma's 13 species all have blue or lavender bowl-shaped flowers that are 5-lobed and borne in coiling spikes. The fruits are dry, papery capsules with few to several seeds. See page 178.

Boraginaceae, borage family

Oklahoma's 24 species of borages are all herbs and are usually hairy or bristly. They bear flowers in uncoiling spikes with all the flowers on one side. The fruits are 4 little nutlets. See pages 179–180.

Verbenaceae, verbena family

There are 23 species in 6 genera of plants in Oklahoma's verbena family. While they are mintlike in habit (including many with square stems), they differ in these ways: the 4 or 5 petal lobes spread to make a not quite symmetrical flower, and the fruits are often berry-like. See pages 181–183.

Lamiaceae, mint family

The Oklahoma mints come in 60 species in 24 genera. Most have square stems with opposite or whorled leaves, and for seeds produce 4 little nutlets (small dry seeds) in the dry remains of the flowers. The usual flower is tubular, with 5 lobes arranged in 2 groups. See pages 184–187.

Solanaceae, tomato family, nightshade family

Oklahoma has 29 species in 7 genera in this family. They vary from edible to poisonous, but all have bell-shaped flowers with 5 points or lobes. The fruits are berries or capsules. See pages 188–189.

Plantaginaceae, plantain family

There are now 20 genera, including 51 species, of the plantain family in Oklahoma. Most of these were formerly placed in the Scrophulariaceae. The flowers are variable, as are the leaves, but all of them have fruits that are dry, papery capsules containing many small dry seeds. Many of them are among the most attractive of our native wildflowers. See pages 190–191.

Orobanchaceae, broomrape family

This family includes fully or partially parasitic plants,

including some of Oklahoma's most common and beautiful wildflowers. Gardeners have been frustrated for years because Indian paintbrush will not grow in their gardens but thrives in the lawn because it is a root parasite on grass. See pages 192–194.

Acanthaceae, acanthus family

In this family, look for bell-shaped flowers on plants with opposite leaves (positioned 2 at a node on the stem). The fruits are capsules. Oklahoma has 7 species in 4 genera of acanthus relatives. A family of worldwide distribution, most members are tropical. See page 195.

Rubiaceae, coffee family

Beginners in flower identification are often surprised to learn that this mostly tropical family has 26 species in Oklahoma. Most are tiny, with small 4-petaled flowers that don't catch the eye but may catch your socks; they are called cleavers. The fruits are dry, papery capsules or single seeds. All have leaves borne in whorls around the stem, sometimes only 2 to a node, and tubular flowers that flare into 4 lobes. See page 196.

Caprifoliaceae, honeysuckle family

The 15 species of the honeysuckle family in Oklahoma are mostly shrubs or woody vines, with plain, opposite leaves and tube-shaped flowers that flare into 5 lobes. The fruits are berry-like. See page 197.

Cucurbitaceae, gourd family

Gourds usually twine or climb and are called vines. The flowers are quite variable but are usually bell-shaped and yellow or white. The leaves are alternate along the stem and usually palmately veined, like maple leaves. The fruits are the typical gourd or melons. Oklahoma hosts 8 species of gourd, 7 of them native and only the occasional cantaloupe as an introduced weed. Most of them are modest and rarely noticed. See pages 198–199.

Campanulaceae, bellflower family

Our bellflowers are usually more mintlike than bell-shaped and often have conspicuous white pollen. The leaves are simple and alternate on the stem, and the fruits are dry capsules bearing many small seeds. Oklahoma hosts 12 species of bellflowers, only 1 of them introduced. The lobelias are the most numerous, with 6 species. They are all plants of wet habitats and thus are more easterly in range. See pages 200–201.

Asteraceae, sunflower family

The sunflower family is the largest family in Oklahoma, with 350 species. That is far too many to show in this book, but here are samples of several of the different tribes. A plant seen in nature might be quite similar to one in the book but not identical. Chances are it is in the same tribe and may then be easily found in a complete flora. See pages 202–216.

Oklahoma Wildflowers

This native plant has leaves that are thrust into the air from submerged roots and are up to 20 inches long. They are broadly arrow-shaped. The inflorescence (part to which the flowers or fruits are attached) is usually longer than the leaves, with several white flowers 1 to 1¼ inches wide. The plants bloom from summer to fall in ditches and along shorelines.

Broadleaf arrowhead, duck potato

Sagittaria latifolia

Big bluestem

Andropogon gerardii

Big bluestem is the defining grass of the Oklahoma tallgrass prairies and native to the state. It occurs statewide, standing 2 to 8 feet tall on prairies, along fence lines and in neglected fields, and along roadsides. A summer grass, it blooms from summer to fall. Look for the turkey-foot shape of the flowering spikes.

Sideoats grama
Bouteloua curtipendula

This beautiful native prairie grass has slender stems that stand 1½ to 5 feet tall on prairies, in parks and old fields, and along roadsides, but seldom in pastures. Sideoats grama can be found in every part of the state, its minute green and orange flowers blooming in the summer.

Buffalo grass

Buchloe dactyloides

Buffalo grass is the signature native grass of the shortgrass prairie. The plants form mats, with the stems only 1 to 8 inches tall. Male and female flowers are on separate plants that often interweave. The male spikes, resembling little flags, are ¼ to ½ inch long. The female spikes are small, short, and held at ground level. The pink and white flowers bloom in April and May.

male spike

female spike

female plant

Switchgrass

Panicum virgatum

One of the "big four" or most important of the tall grasses that traditionally define a prairie as tallgrass, this beautiful native plant grows in large clumps 2 to 7 feet tall on prairies, in fencerows, and along roadsides statewide. The panicles are open, 8 to 12 inches long, and produced in profusion during the late summer to fall. Flowers are green, pink, and orange.

Little bluestem

Schizachyrium scoparium

Little bluestem, possibly the most common native grass in the state, grows wild in every county and is an essential component of drier sites on the tallgrass and midgrass prairies. The stems are clumping and about 16 to 40 inches tall. The small flowering spikes, green and yellow, are solitary in each upper leaf node and ¾ inch to 2¼ inches long, blooming from July to September.

Indiangrass

Sorghastrum nutans

The Oklahoma state legislature has designated Indiangrass the official Oklahoma state grass. A native plant, it is one of the major grasses of the tallgrass prairie. While it does best in deep, fertile soils, Indiangrass can be found in every part of Oklahoma. The stems grow from 3 to 8 feet tall, with the inflorescences 6 to 12 inches long, and bloom from September through October. Look for a swath of misty blue stems bearing flowers that appear to be made of gold and silver.

Hop sedge

Carex lupulina

The green to light brown flowering stems of this native plant grow singly or crowded in very wet habitats such as ditches, along riverbanks, and along lakeshores of the eastern third of Oklahoma. Stems are stout and 8 inches to 5 feet tall. The fruiting spikes, packed in masses of 4 to 6 in clusters 4 or 5 inches long, bloom in May and June.

A native Oklahoma plant, sand spikerush grows on sandy floodplains and in creek beds and ditches of the entire state except the Panhandle. It is probably the most common spikerush in the state, its dense mats of rhizomes—horizontal underground stems—packing the surfaces of sandy shorelines. The spikes are ⅛ to ¾ inch long on erect stems 4 to 20 inches high and bloom green and brown from April to June.

Sand spikerush

Eleocharis montevidensis

Great bulrush, hardstem bulrush

Schoenoplectus acutus

The stems are erect, round in cross section, and 4 to 20 feet tall. This native plant grows in sloughs, fresh or brackish marshes, ponds, or along lakeshores over the entire state. The flower spikes are each ½ to ¾ inch long and are borne in tight, stiff clusters. They bloom green and light brown from late spring through summer.

Fringed nutrush
Scleria ciliata

Stems are single or tufted, erect, and 8 to 29 inches tall. This native plant grows on prairies and in forest openings of the eastern three-quarters of Oklahoma. The clusters of small green flowers, about ⅛ to ½ inch long, bloom from April through September, their blooming period being affected by seasonal rainfall.

Green dragon, dragonroot

Arisaema dracontium

These native plants are 1 to 2 feet tall and grow in mostly shady forest environments in the eastern three-quarters of the state. The inflorescences (parts to which flowers or fruits are attached) are 3 to 10 inches long, including the long slender tip. The plants bloom in May. The showy red fruits are a favorite of birds.

flower spike

Yelloweyed grass

Xyris torta

The thin flexible stems of this native plant rise 3 to 40 inches from bogs and shallow pond margins in the eastern half of Oklahoma. The yellow flowers are about ½ inch across and bloom in June to August.

Slender dayflower

Commelina erecta

There is a garden weed that looks very much like this graceful native, but this plant is well-behaved and lives in sandy or rocky soils in all parts of Oklahoma. The plants are 1 to 3 feet tall. The flowers are ¾ to 1 inch across and bloom from May to October. Note the tiny white third petal below the two blue ones.

The erect stems are often branched, smooth, and 2 to 3 feet tall. This native plant grows statewide on sandy or rocky prairies, in open woods, and in disturbed sites. Inch-wide blue flowers are produced from April through July, weather permitting.

Ohio spiderwort

Tradescantia ohiensis

Pickerelweed, water hyacinth

Pontederia cordata

A common large plant of lake margins and ponds of the eastern three-quarters of the state, native pickerelweed emerges from roots in mud to 2 to 3 feet above water level. The blue-purple flower spikes are 3 to 6 inches long and bloom from May to October.

Stems are erect, 8 to 28 inches long, and grow on stream and lake margins, in marshes, on wet prairies, and in ditches statewide except the Panhandle. The inflorescence (part to which flower or fruit is attached) of this native plant is branched, many-flowered, and produced from June through October. Flowers are brown and green.

Grassleaf rush

Juncus marginatus

Woodrush

Luzula bulbosa

Stems are solitary or in small tufts, 3 to 16 inches tall, and grow in open woods and fields of the entire state, usually not far from water. The inflorescences are about ½ inch long and bloom brown and green from April to June. The plant is native to Oklahoma.

Wild onion, wild garlic

Allium canadense

This is a very common native spring flower seen along roadsides, on prairies, and in parks, fields, and disturbed sites statewide except the Panhandle. It is quite variable; sometimes little bulblets like garlic cloves are produced instead of some or all of the flowers. The plants are about 6 to 12 inches tall. The flower heads are 2 to 3 inches across and bloom pink to white in March to early June. All but one of our *Allium* species have the characteristic onion or garlic odor.

Funnel lily

Androstephium coeruleum

These are little, early spring native lilies of the prairies, especially rocky ones, and are found statewide except in the Panhandle. The stems are ½ inch to 7 inches tall and bear 2 to 9 pale blue or white flowers, each ¾ inch to 1¼ inches wide. They bloom from April to May.

The stems of this native plant grow 1 to 2 feet tall on prairies, especially rocky ones, in the eastern three-quarters of Oklahoma. The flowering portion is 3 to 7 inches long with white to blue-violet flowers that are about ¼ to ½ inch long and bloom from April to June.

Eastern camass, wild hyacinth

Camassia scilloides

White dog's tooth violet, white trout lily

Erythronium albidum

Producing early spring flowers, these native plants rise 3 to 8 inches high in March or April on prairies, in forest openings, and in cemeteries of the eastern three-quarters of Oklahoma. The pendulous white flowers are about 1½ inches long.

Summer spider lily

Hymenocallis caroliniana

The flowering stems of this native plant are 1 to 2½ feet tall and grow in forest openings on damp sand in the easternmost quarter of Oklahoma. The white flowers are about 8 inches across and bloom from May through August.

Yellow stargrass

Hypoxis hirsuta

Small hairy native plants that grow on prairies and in open woods over the eastern three-quarters of Oklahoma, they are 3 to 12 inches tall. The yellow flowers are ½ to 1 inch wide and bloom from April to July.

This poisonous onionlike plant is common in lawns and pastures, on prairies, and in forest openings of the eastern three-quarters of Oklahoma. It does not have an oniony odor, and the flowers are more yellowish than those of onions. These native plants are 4 to 30 inches tall, and each little flower is about ¼ to ½ inch long and white to yellowish white. Plants bloom from April to May and sometimes again in the fall.

Crow-poison, false garlic

Nothoscordum bivalve

Green trillium

Trillium viridescens

Plants are erect, 8 to 20 inches tall, and found on moist forest floors of the eastern third of Oklahoma. There are several varieties, some with leaves streaked with purple, most with purplish flowers. The flowers of this native plant are about 1½ to 2½ inches long and bloom in March and April.

Native to the eastern edges of Oklahoma and naturalized in the eastern half of the state, blue flag grows in seeps, bogs, marshes, and ditches where the ground is always wet. The plants are 2½ to 3½ feet tall when in bloom. The violet or blue flowers are 3 or 4 inches wide and bloom from April to June.

Southern blue flag, bog-iris

Iris virginica

Celestial lily, prairie iris

Nemastylis geminiflora

True prairie-lovers, these native plants spring 6 to 20 inches tall from a deep bulb on prairies of the eastern half of Oklahoma. The blue, lavender, or orchid flowers are usually borne in twos, each about 1½ inches wide, and bloom in late March through April. Look for them early in the next spring after a prairie fire.

The bright green leaves and stems of this native plant are spreading, about 5 to 18 inches long, and grow on prairies, lawns, and roadsides of the eastern three-quarters of Oklahoma. The blue to violet flowers are about ½ inch wide and bloom in April and May.

Blue-eyed grass

Sisyrinchium angustifolium

Oklahoma grass-pink

Calopogon oklahomensis

Found on moist prairies of the eastern third of Oklahoma and in scattered locations in the south, these native plants grow 5 to 8 inches tall, usually in well-spaced colonies. The pink to orchid flowers are about 1 inch wide and bloom in April and May.

Photos: Jim Norman

Known in Oklahoma only from the Ouachita Mountains of the southeastern corner of the state, this native orchid grows 1 to 2 feet tall in dense wet forests on stony hillsides. The flowers are 2 to 4 inches long and bloom in May.

Yellow lady's slipper

Cypripedium kentuckiense

Chatterbox

Epipactis gigantea

On stems 1 to 3 feet tall, these native plants grow in dense brush or forest near water in the Arbuckle Mountains of south-central Oklahoma and in a few widely scattered sites from California to British Columbia. The orange flowers with purple streaks are about 1 inch long and bloom in June and July.

The showiest of Oklahoma's orchids, these native plants grow in swamps of the southeastern corner of the state. The stems are 2 to 4 feet tall, always growing in stands of ferns. The panicles (many-branched inflorescences) are 2 to 10 inches high and bloom in August.

Yellow fringed orchid

Platanthera ciliaris

Photos: Jim Norman

Great Plains ladies' tress

Spiranthes magnicamporum

The stems are stout, 8 to 24 inches tall, and grow on wet prairies and in ditches (and the occasional parking lot) in central, south-central, and southwestern Oklahoma. The white or cream flowers are intensely vanilla scented and about ½ inch long. They bloom from September until frost.

Three-birds orchid, nodding pogonia

Triphora trianthophora

These native plants are hard to find, growing along streams in the leaf litter of dense forests in southeastern counties, the Caddo Canyons, and the Arbuckle Mountains. The stems are 3 to 10 inches long and upright to ascending. The white flowers are about ¾ inch wide and bloom from August to September.

Annual buckwheat

Eriogonum annuum

Erect stems, unbranched to the inflorescence (the part to which the flowers are attached), are 4 to 50 inches tall and found on sunny, sandy, or stony prairie soils of the western two-thirds of Oklahoma, occasionally also in the east-central area. The many tiny white and pink flowers of this native plant are densely packed in branched inflorescences 4 to 11 inches wide and bloom from July through September.

Pretty enough to be put in a flower garden, this erect, branching native plant grows 2 to 5 feet tall in barrow ditches, fields, and along roadsides statewide. The spikes are cylindrical, blunt-tipped, 1 to 3 inches long, and about ¾ inch thick. The pink flowers bloom from June to October.

Pennsylvania smartweed, pinkweed

Polygonum pensylvanicum

Pale dock, tall dock

Rumex altissimus

The erect stems of dock, a native plant, rise usually unbranched 1 to 3 feet high in pastures, fields, and along roadsides statewide. The inflorescence (part to which flowers are attached) is 1 inch to nearly 12 inches long, blooming from April to July.

From woody taproots, the stems of this native plant rise 3 to 4 feet tall, growing on sandy or rocky soils in pastures and on roadsides of the entire state. The orchid to pink flowers are about ½ inch long, night-blooming, and occur from June to September.

Smooth four o'clock

Mirabilis glabra

Spring beauty

Claytonia virginica

Rising only 4 to 16 inches high, spring beauty is a spring ephemeral of forests, but this native plant has made its way into lawns, parks, and other sheltered areas over the entire state. It prefers rocky or clay soils. The pink or white flowers are ¾ to 1 inch across and bloom from February to June.

Slender stems 1 to 4 inches high rise from a whorl of fleshy leaves in dry, rocky or sandy soils of the eastern three-quarters of Oklahoma. The pink to rose flowers are ¾ to 1 inch across and bloom in May and June, but only when the sun is shining.

Rock-pink, flame flower, flower-of-an-hour

Talinum calycinum

Clammy chickweed

Cerastium glomeratum

These introduced plants are annuals, 2 to 12 inches tall, sometimes branched, sometimes decumbent. They grow on sandy or rocky soils in disturbed sites over the eastern three-quarters of Oklahoma. The white flowers are about ½ inch wide, deeply notched at the petal tips, and bloom in April.

Drummond's sandwort

Minuartia drummondii

These native plants are annuals with stems 2 to 8 inches high and leaves nearly linear or grasslike. Drummond's sandwort grows on sandy prairies, in pastures, and in woodland openings in the eastern two-thirds of Oklahoma. The showy white flowers are ¾ to 1 inch across and bloom from April to May.

Fire-pink

Silene virginica

A native forest plant, fire-pink rises 1 to 2 feet high under trees on rocky soils of the Ozark and Ouachita Mountains. The red flowers are about 1 inch across and bloom from April to June.

Common chickweed, ten-petal

Stellaria media

These are low, mat-forming plants that may be evergreen in sheltered areas. The stems are 3 to 20 inches long, often branched, and grow as weeds in flower beds, lawns, gardens, and waste places over the eastern three-quarters of Oklahoma. The white flowers of this introduced species are ¼ to ½ inch wide and may bloom any time from January to December, with a flush in March.

American lotus

Nelumbo lutea

Scattered in lakes and ponds of the eastern three-fourths of Oklahoma, the native *Nelumbo* is rooted in the mud and has both floating and emergent leaves. The emergent flowers are 6 to 10 inches wide, yellow, and bloom from June to September.

Prairie anemone, Carolina anemone

Anemone caroliniana

On stems 2 to 9 inches tall, anemones spring up in pastures, prairies, and meadows (but not along roadsides or in fields, which are disturbed land) statewide except in the Panhandle. The white or blue flowers of this native plant are ¾ inch to 1¾ inches across and bloom from March to April.

blue color variation

white color variation

Rue anemone

Anemonella thalictroides

The stems of this native plant are 3 to 12 inches tall and very common on forest floors of the eastern third of the state. The white or orchid flowers are ½ to 1 inch wide and bloom from March to May.

The branching stems of this native plant are 1 to 3 feet tall and grow in forested sites in the eastern third of Oklahoma. The pink to red flowers are 1 to 2 inches long and bloom from April to June. They make fine garden flowers in partial shade when started from seed.

Wild columbine, red columbine

Aquilegia canadensis

Leather flower, blue bell, Pitcher's clematis

Clematis pitcheri

These native plants are vines, sometimes woody at the base, with stems 1 to 20 feet long. They grow in the wet soils of ditches and creek bottoms statewide except in the northwestern quarter and the Panhandle. The blue-violet flowers are without petals, having showy, thick, leathery sepals instead, and are about ½ to 1½ inches long, blooming from June through July. The flowers are followed by flat, nearly round seeds with feathery tails.

White water crowfoot

Ranunculus aquatilis

The stems of this native plant grow floating in the water of slow-moving streams or ponds and are 12 to 32 inches long. The plants are found in widely scattered locations statewide. The little ½-inch white flowers bloom on emergent stems from April to August.

Early buttercup, prairie buttercup

Ranunculus fascicularis

The stems of this native plant grow 2 to 12 inches tall and are common on prairies and in dry forest openings in the eastern half of the state and in Cotton County. The yellow flowers are ½ to 1 inch wide and bloom from March to May.

The sturdy stems of these native plants grow 2 to 7 feet tall on creek banks, in ravines, and in other wet, shaded sites in the eastern half of Oklahoma. The flowers are only about ¼ inch long but are produced in large panicles (many-branched inflorescences) that bloom from June to July.

Purple meadow rue

Thalictrum dasycarpum

Prickly poppy

Argemone polyanthemos

The erect stems of this native plant rise 1½ to 5 feet tall on mostly sandy soils of prairies and floodplains and along roadsides in the western half of Oklahoma and in a few sites in the northeastern quarter. The plants are often mistaken for thistles because of the very prickly leaves. The sap is opaque, thick, and bright yellow. White flowers 2 to 4 inches long bloom from May to August.

Bloodroot

Sanguinaria canadensis

This attractive little native plant gets its common name from its thick, blood-red sap. The flowers rise only 3 to 8 inches on leafless stems from a whorl of leaves at the base. The plants are found in leaf litter on wooded hills in the eastern third of Oklahoma. The white flowers are 1 to 2 inches wide and bloom from March to May.

Golden corydalis, scrambled eggs

Corydalis aurea

Arching or prostrate stems 4 to 20 inches long grow on sunny, sandy soils of prairies in the western two-thirds of Oklahoma. The yellow flowers of this native plant are ½ to ¾ inch long and bloom from March to May.

Stems are 4 to 16 inches long and weak and pliable, flowing over the soil and other plants. This native plant may be found on sunny prairies and in pastures of the eastern half of Oklahoma. Yellow flowers ½ to ¾ inch long bloom from March to May.

Mealy corydalis

Corydalis crystallina

Dutchman's breeches

Dicentra cucullaria

These charming native plants are usually found in leaf litter and along trails in the forests of northeastern Oklahoma. Their stems rise 2 to 12 inches from the cluster of basal leaves. The white or pale pink flowers are about ½ inch long and bloom in March and April.

Found in waste places, roadsides, lawns, and gardens statewide, shepherd's purse grows 4 to 24 inches tall with leaves that clasp the stems and heart-shaped seed pods that give this introduced plant its common name. The white flowers are about ⅛ inch long and bloom from March to May.

Shepherd's purse

Capsella bursa-pastoris

Toothwort, toothcup

Cardamine concatenata

Found in moist, forested areas of northeastern Oklahoma, these native plants are just a few inches high and topped by drooping clusters of ½-inch white or pink flowers that bloom in March and April.

Spectacle-pod

Dimorphocarpa candicans

This attractive native plant, found in western Oklahoma, is often collected for gardens but needs sandy soil and full sun to survive. The stems are 1 to 3 feet tall. Clusters of ½-inch white flowers appear from May to September. The common name refers to the seed pods, which are shaped like eyeglasses.

Photos: Jim Norman

Western wallflower, plains wallflower

Erysimum asperum

The erect stems of this native plant are 8 to 30 inches high and can be found in dunes, on prairies, and in thickets in the western two-thirds of Oklahoma. The showy flowers are ¾ to 1½ inches wide and bloom from March through May.

Golden glade-cress

Leavenworthia aurea

This tiny native plant, only 1 to 3 inches high, is found in a few limestone glades of McCurtain and Choctaw Counties. The yellow flowers are about ¼ inch long and bloom in March and April. This glade habitat is worth exploring for many other unusual and beautiful plants.

Spreading bladderpod, cloth-of-gold

Lesquerella gracilis

These native plants grow 4 to 20 inches high or long on any soils of prairies, pastures, and roadsides, scattered statewide except in the Panhandle and north-central areas. The yellow or white flowers are about ½ inch long and bloom from March to June.

western color variation

Stems 2 to 5 feet tall grow on deep sandy soils of the western half of Oklahoma except the Panhandle. The flowers are about ½ to ¾ inch long and of mixed colors, purple, pink, or orchid to white. They bloom from April to July.

Smooth twistflower, jewelweed

Streptanthus hyacinthoides

Rocky Mountain beeplant

Cleome serrulata

An erect, branching plant 1 to 6 feet tall, beeplant grows on the disturbed soils of prairies and pastures in the western third of Oklahoma and in a few sites in the northeastern corner. The white to orchid or pink flowers, ¾ to 1 inch long, of this native plant bloom from July to October.

Roughseed clammyweed

Polanisia dodecandra

Clammyweed stems grow 8 to 30 inches high or long on sandy or gravelly soils in waste places, along roadsides, and in dry streambeds statewide. The pink to rose flowers of this native plant are about ¾ inch long and may bloom from June through September.

Yellow stonecrop

Sedum nuttallianum

Yellow stonecrop, a native plant, appears in rocky sites that may occur anywhere in Oklahoma, including the Panhandle, but has not been collected in the northwestern corner. This low plant has branching stems 1½ to 5 inches high or long and bears many ¼-inch yellow flowers from late spring to early summer.

You may find pink stonecrop on dry, rocky or sandy soils in the eastern half of Oklahoma. The stems of this native plant are ascending, 4 to 12 inches long, and bear ¼-inch pink flowers on 4 or 5 branches about 1 to 2½ inches long from April to June. Sometimes the flowers are so pale as to appear white.

Widow's cross, pink stonecrop

Sedum pulchellum

Wild strawberry

Fragaria virginiana

These native woodland plants grow 2 to 8 inches high in moist, shady sites statewide except the northwestern sector and the Panhandle. The white flowers are about ½ to ¾ inch wide, blooming in April and May, and are followed by tiny, tasty fruit, if you can beat the wild creatures to them.

White avens, redroot
Geum canadense

The stems of this native plant are ascending, 1 to 3 feet tall, and are common in forested areas and gardens statewide, with the exception of the Panhandle and the extreme southwestern corner. The white flowers are about ½ inch wide and may bloom from May to July. They are followed by the strange, burlike ball fruits bristling with little hooks.

Five finger, old-field cinquefoil

Potentilla simplex

The spreading or ascending stems are 8 to 22 inches long, rooting at the tips to form new colonies. This native plant is found in forest openings, on prairies, and in old fields in the eastern half of Oklahoma and the Panhandle. The yellow flowers are ½ to ¾ inch wide and bloom from April to June. Five finger makes a lovely ground cover for shady lawns where enough moisture can be provided.

Pasture rose

Rosa carolina

The long, slender stems of pasture rose rise unbranched 8 to 40 inches high on prairies, in open woodlands, and along roadsides of the eastern half of Oklahoma. The usually pink flowers of this native species are about 2 to 3 inches across and are borne singly or in twos or threes from April through June.

Pasture rose should not be mistaken for the noxious weed *Rosa multiflora*, multiflora rose, which has been introduced to feed wildlife and is taking over pastures and woodlands statewide. *Rosa multiflora* bears its smaller flowers in clumps of about a dozen.

Southern dewberry

Rubus trivialis

With stems that are trailing to arching, canes rooting at the tips, and 2 to 5 feet long, this common native blackberry grows in waste places, pastures, fencerows, and along roadsides in the eastern, central, and southwestern sections of Oklahoma. White flowers 1 to 2 inches wide appear in April and May and are followed by the sweet black aggregate fruits in June.

Prairie acacia
Acacia angustissima

Clump-forming stems about 1 to 2 feet tall grow on dry, rocky or sandy soils in pastures and prairies statewide except the far northwestern and southeastern corners. The many tiny white flowers of this native plant are obscured by the long silky anthers and are borne in tight round clusters in the summer.

Illinois bundleflower

Desmanthus illinoensis

Stems are erect or nearly so, growing 1 to 6 feet high, and are found on roadsides, in openings in woodlands, and in pastures statewide. The small white flowers of this native plant are obscured by the typical ½- to ¾-inch balls of whitish stamens. Blooming is from June through July. The pods are brown and twisted into the tight, rounded balls often called wood roses.

Sensitive briar, catclaw

Mimosa quadrivalvis

Botanists have had a hard time deciding which of the many names this beautiful little native plant has acquired should become the official name, so if you learned it as *Schrankia nuttallii*, you're still right. Sprawling, mat-forming plants with stems 2 to 4 feet long grow in waste places, on road banks, and in ravines statewide. The bright balls of showy anthers appear from May to July and are followed by scary-looking prickly pods. The stems are armed with hooked prickles.

Yellow puff, neptunia

Neptunia lutea

Stems are prostrate, about 2 to 6 feet long, and unarmed. This native plant is found on prairies, along roadsides, and in waste places statewide except in the northwestern sector and the Panhandle. The flowering spikes are oblong rather than round, about 1 inch long, with the yellow flowers obscured by the long anthers. The plants bloom in June and July.

The stems of this native plant grow 4 to 18 inches long on dry, rocky and gravelly soils of the western two-thirds of Oklahoma, especially in the Panhandle. The yellow flowers are ¼ to ½ inch long, borne among the leaves, and they bloom from May to August. Several states have listed this plant as a noxious weed.

James' rush-pea

Caesalpinia jamesii

Partridge pea

Chamaecrista fasciculata

A showy native plant of roadsides and pastures, this 4- to 50-inch-tall plant grows statewide. The yellow flowers are twisted in appearance and 1 inch or a little more in length. They bloom from June to September.

Wild senna

Senna marilandica

Erect stems 2 to 6 feet tall grow along creek banks and in riverside thickets and other moist sites, scattered statewide except in the Panhandle. The yellow flowers of this native plant are ½ to 1 inch long and bloom from June to August. They are followed by long black pods with each seed pinched into a separate pocket.

Leadplant

Amorpha canescens

This native plant grows on prairie soils, in fields, and along roadsides of the entire state except the southeastern corner. A small shrub, 1 to 6 feet tall, it produces finger-sized spikes of small, 1-petaled purple flowers from April to August. Leadplant is eagerly grazed and is seldom to be found in grazed pasturelands.

American ground nut

Apios americana

The climbing, twining vines of this native plant reach 3 to 16 feet in moist thickets along pond and stream banks of the eastern, central, and southwestern parts of Oklahoma. Drooping clusters of brownish red-purple and white ½- to ¾-inch flowers appear from June to August, but rarely set fruit. The roots produce many 1- to 2½-inch potato-like tubers, which are edible.

Missouri milkvetch

Astragalus missouriensis

Stems are 4 to 20 inches long and upright or spreading. This native plant is found mostly on prairie soils of roadsides, hills, and pastures in the western and central parts of the state, especially in the Panhandle. The purple, orchid, or pink to white flowers are each about ½ inch long and form clusters of 6 to 16, blooming from April through June.

Southern indigo, wild blue indigo

Baptisia australis

On stems 1 to 4 feet tall, these native plants grow in rocky or gravelly sites statewide except in the Panhandle. The flowers, each about ¾ inch long, are borne in long clusters of 4 to 40 flowers in April to July. In the Wichita Mountains, hybrids of *Baptisia australis* and *Baptisia sphaerocarpa*, yellow wild indigo, which has yellow flowers, produce stands of multicolored flowers.

Butterfly pea, pigeon's wings

Clitoria mariana

The slender stems of this native plant trail 8 to 30 inches in lightly wooded, sandy or rocky areas of the eastern half and southwestern part of Oklahoma. The orchid flowers, 1½ to 2½ inches long, often appear in twos. They bloom from May through September.

Golden prairie clover, silktop

Dalea aurea

These native plants grow on stems 8 to 30 inches tall on prairie soils of pastures, hillsides, and ravines in the western two-thirds of Oklahoma. The dense spikes of small yellow flowers are ¾ inch to 3½ inches long. They bloom from June to August.

Purple prairie clover

Dalea purpurea

Many-stemmed plants 8 to 30 inches tall and erect or spreading, these natives grow on dry, rocky or sandy soils on prairies statewide. They are enjoyed by grazing animals and so are seldom found in pastures. The many tiny purple to violet flowers are borne on narrow spikes ½ inch to 3 inches long from May to August.

Sticky tickclover, large-flowered tickclover

Desmodium glutinosum

The erect stems of this native plant, 15 to 40 inches tall, are found in forest clearings statewide except the Panhandle. A single whorl of several 3-part leaves appears at about the middle or sometimes near the base of the stem. Pink flowers, about ¼ inch long, bloom from June to August. The seeds resemble small brown beans and are eagerly eaten by wildlife.

Bladderpod

Sesbania vesicaria

Tall, spare, branching plants from 2 to 7 feet high, this native species is found in mostly sandy pastures of the central and south-central areas of Oklahoma. The fruits are poisonous, and livestock avoid them when other food is available. Orange or sometimes yellow to red flowers are ¼ to ½ inch long, dangling in few-flowered clusters from July to October.

Western indigo, scarlet pea

Indigofera miniata

The stems of this native plant are usually sprawling, 4 inches to 4 feet long, and found in rocky or sandy prairie openings in the western half of the state or scattered in the eastern half. The rather showy, pink to red flowers are about ½ to ¾ inch long and borne in small clusters. They bloom from May through August.

Bush clover, round-head lespedeza

Lespedeza capitata

The stems of this native plant reach 2 to 7 feet tall and are found in old fields, along roadsides, and on prairies statewide except in the Panhandle. The purple to pink flowers, each about ¼ inch long, are borne in rounded clumps toward the top of the stem from August to October. Bush clover makes a good forage plant for grazing animals.

Yellow melilot, yellow sweet-clover

Melilotus officinalis

This plant and the very similar white-flowered species are introductions from Europe but have made themselves at home in the United States. The plants are 2 to 6 feet tall, branched, and common statewide in pastures, along roads, and in waste places. The tiny yellow flowers are borne on spikes 2 to 6 inches long and bloom from May to October. In the still morning air, their fragrance is wonderful.

Purple locoweed, crazyweed

Oxytropis lambertii

These native plants are 2 to 12 inches tall when in bloom and may be found on prairies, on plains, and along roadsides in the western two-thirds of Oklahoma. The magenta to purple flowers are ¾ inch long, arranged in cylindrical spikes of 10 to 25 flowers, and bloom from April to May. Where selenium is present in the soil, *Oxytropis* is poisonous to livestock.

Tallbread scurf-pea

Pediomelum cuspidatum

With stems that lean or lie among the neighbors and 1 to 2 feet long, this native plant is found on dry prairies, along gravelly banks, and in creek valleys in the western three-quarters of Oklahoma. They have a superficial resemblance to bluebonnet (*Lupinus*) flowers. The individual blue to purple flowers are about ½ to ¾ inch long and are borne in broad clusters of 25 to 40 flowers, blooming from May to July.

Wild bean, amberique bean

Strophostyles helvola

Trailing or twining vines 1 to 7 feet long grow on other vegetation or fences statewide except in the Panhandle. The pink to white flowers of this native plant are about ½ inch long and are usually borne singly or in pairs, blooming from June to October. They produce small pods resembling green beans, but the seeds are densely stiff-hairy and unpalatable.

Goat's rue

Tephrosia virginiana

The stems of goat's rue, usually several emerging from a common base, grow 8 to 30 inches high on sandy soils of dunes and along roadsides statewide except in the Panhandle. The showy clusters of tricolored (yellow, pink, and orchid) ¾-inch flowers bloom from May to July. This species is native to Oklahoma.

White clover

Trifolium repens

White clover is a mat-forming plant with creeping stems that root at the nodes and are 4 to 18 inches long. Plants grow in lawns, in pastures, and along roadsides statewide from April to June. The heads are ½ to 1½ inches in diameter. White clover was introduced early in the settlement of the United States from Europe to improve pastures and provide a source of honey.

Hairy vetch, woollypod vetch, winter vetch

Vicia villosa

This vetch, an introduced species, was planted along roadsides and escaped into pastures and fields statewide except in the Panhandle. The stems are 2 to 6 feet long, climbing by tendrils. Narrow, cylindrical, purple to blue flowers, about ½ inch long, are borne in long spikes of 40 to 60 flowers and bloom from April to July.

Trailing ratany

Krameria lanceolata

The stems of trailing ratany sprawl on the ground in the western two-thirds of Oklahoma and are 8 to 30 inches long. The intricate, ½- to ¾-inch magenta flowers bloom from May to July. The flower should be viewed with a magnifying glass to appreciate its beauty. The fruit is a small, 1-seeded pod with sharp prickles.

Stork's bill, filaria
Erodium cicutarium

The weak, nearly prostrate stems of this introduced species are only 2 to 3 inches high at flowering but become as much as 20 inches long in fruit. They are scattered in lawns and waste places over the body of the state. Purple to magenta flowers, ¼ to ½ inch wide, appear from February to June. Originally from Europe, this is probably a garden plant that has made itself at home here.

Cranesbill

Geranium carolinianum

Cranesbill is native to Oklahoma. The stems are erect to ascending, often-branched, and 4 to 30 inches long. They may be found along roadsides, in waste places, and in gardens over the body of the state. The pale pink to white, ¼- to ⅜-inch flowers bloom from April to June. They are followed by the characteristic beaked capsules, thought to resemble a bird's bill.

Weak stems about 4 to 20 inches long lean on other plants in forest openings, on prairies, and in wastelands, and are found scattered statewide. The flowers of this native species range in color from almost orange or yellow to pale green. Flowers are about ½ inch wide and bloom from May to June.

Sheep sour, yellow wood sorrel

Oxalis stricta

Violet wood sorrel

Oxalis violacea

Leaves that are green above and bright purple below rise without a common stem 5 to 12 inches high in open woods, on prairies, and along roadsides statewide except in the Panhandle. The species is native to Oklahoma. The orchid to purple flowers are about ¾ inch wide and bloom twice, in April to May and again in September to October.

Prairie flax, blue flax
Linum pratense

The slender stems of this native herb are branched near the base and 8 to 30 inches tall. They are found on prairies and lightly wooded hills statewide, but in scattered locations. The blue flowers bloom from April to June.

Stiffstem flax, prairie flax

Linum rigidum

Stiffstem flax may be found anywhere in the state on prairie soils except in the Arkansas River valley, from April to June. The slender stems are 2 to 20 inches tall, with yellow flowers ¾ inch to 1¼ inches long borne singly at the tips. These native plants are a favorite of roadside-planting projects.

Grooved flax

Linum sulcatum

This modest little native plant grows 8 to 20 inches tall, blooming in pastures and Cross Timbers clearings statewide except in the northwestern quarter and the Panhandle. The yellow flowers are ½ to ¾ inch long and bloom from May to July.

White milkwort

Polygala alba

whorled milkwort

Slim, unbranched stems 4 to 16 inches high form byway bouquets on prairie hills and in scrublands of the western half of Oklahoma. The tiny green-centered white flowers form dense spikes ½ to 1 inch long in May to July. In northeastern Oklahoma is found our other white *Polygala*, *Polygala verticillata*, whorled milkwort, a bit taller than *Polygala alba* and occurring in dry, sandy or rocky sites from May to August.

Usually only 1 slender stem, 4 to 20 inches high, bears a single spike about ⅓ inch wide and ¾ inch to 1½ inches long. Found in sandy prairie openings of the eastern two-thirds of Oklahoma, this native species blooms from May to August. *Polygala polygama*, bitter milkwort, another member of the genus, resembles a small pink clover, growing on damp sandy or boggy soils of the southeastern quarter of Oklahoma. It blooms from May to June.

Slender milkwort, pink milkwort

Polygala incarnata

bitter milkwort

Spotted spurge, prostrate milk spurge

Chamaesyce maculata

A mat-making plant with stems 2 to 18 inches long, spotted spurge grows statewide except for the Panhandle. It may be found in disturbed sites along roads and in parks. The native plants are covered with a grayish coat of fuzz that shows well the clumps of tiny white to pinkish flowers and fruits from June to October.

Bull-nettle
Cnidoscolus texanus

This native plant is not a true nettle at all, but it stings like one! Stout stems 1 to 3 feet tall grow on deep sandy soils of the central and southern parts of Oklahoma, particularly in pastures. The showy white, fragrant flowers are 1 to 2 inches long and wide (and they sting, too!). Bull-nettle blooms from May to September.

Hogwort, wooly croton

Croton capitatus

Plants stand 1 to 3 feet tall and are covered with star-shaped hairs. This native plant is usually found growing on dry, sandy, or gypsum prairie soils statewide. The tiny white to green flowers covered with brownish hairs bloom from June through September.

Snow-on-the-mountain

Euphorbia marginata

Statewide, this showy native plant, 1 to 3 feet tall, decorates overgrazed pastures and wastelands with its white to green flowers from July to October. It is poisonous to some people, much like poison ivy, and so should be handled with care. Often, snow-on-the-mountain is the only plant left standing in a dry pasture at the end of the season.

Noseburn

Tragia ramosa

Another stinging, nettlelike plant, 4 to 12 inches tall, noseburn is found growing on many soils and rocky slopes scattered over southwestern Oklahoma. The minute green flowers bloom from May to October. Noseburn's strange name is derived from the inflammation it causes in grazing animals that encounter this native plant among their forage plants.

Purple poppy mallow, winecups

Callirhoe involucrata

Stems are sprawling, 8 to 30 inches long, and are found on dry, usually sandy soil of prairies and plains and forest openings in the central, southwestern, and southeastern areas of Oklahoma. The purple to magenta, rarely white, flowers are 1¼ to 2 inches wide, borne singly, and bloom from April to August. The small green fruits of this native plant make a tasty nibble.

Scarlet globe mallow

Sphaeralcea coccinea

On stems that are wooly and erect or ascending, 1 to 2 feet long, globe mallows grow on the dry prairies and plains of the western three-quarters of Oklahoma. The red to orange flowers of this native plant are individually about 1 inch wide and are borne in clusters, blooming from May to October.

Nits-and-lice

Hypericum drummondii

On stems 4 to 14 inches high and unbranched below the flowers, this little summer wildflower blooms in lightly wooded areas and old fields of the eastern half of state and in Comanche County. Look for the fan-blade shape of the soft yellow flowers, ⅛ to ¼ inch long. Nits-and-lice blooms from July to September, with a peak in August.

Common St. John's-wort, Klamath weed

Hypericum perforatum

An introduced weed of cultivated fields and roadsides, this upright, shrubby plant is found statewide except in the Panhandle. The masses of small, bright yellow flowers bloom from May to August. This is a European plant but is much more common than the native shrubby St. John's-wort.

Nodding green violet
Hybanthus verticillatus

Usually found on rocky prairie soils, nodding green violet has upright branched stems 1 to 3 feet tall, bearing a few small, green to pinkish brown flowers ⅛ to ¼ inch long. The flowers are hard to see because of their color and position, and do not much resemble woods violets. They are found in the western half of Oklahoma, in the southeastern quarter, and in Tulsa County. They bloom from April to July. This plant is native to Oklahoma.

Johnny-jump-up, field pansy

Viola bicolor

This tiny native annual is very common in lawns and along roadsides statewide except in the far northwestern sector and the Panhandle. The plants are only about 2 to 5 inches tall but are produced in such profusion that they are easily visible from a moving vehicle. They bloom in March through April. The white to blue or violet flowers are ½ inch wide or less.

Bird's-foot violet
Viola pedata

A few deeply lobed leaves in the leaf litter support stems 2 to 5 inches high, each with 1 pansy-like flower 1 to 1½ inches wide. The colors are very variable, ranging from white to blue, orchid, or purple; often in a population no two will be exactly alike. These native plants grow in rocky forest openings and along roadsides in forested areas. In Oklahoma they are found in the eastern half of the state, blooming from March to May.

Butterfly violet, meadow violet

Viola sororia

This very common blue violet may be found in wooded or brushy places statewide. Plants are 2 to 8 inches high, with white to orchid or violet flowers ½ to ¾ inch wide, held well above the heart-shaped leaves. These native plants bloom from March to May and occasionally until frost.

Passion flower, May-pop

Passiflora incarnata

Vigorous vines with 3-lobed leaves grow 4 to 25 feet long on prairie soils of the eastern half of Oklahoma, climbing on shrubs or fences, but often just making lovely mounds on open ground. The big, 2- to 3-inch, exotic-looking flowers are usually some shade of lavender purple but may be white or blue as well. The edible gourdlike fruits of this native plant are about the size and shape of a hen's egg. They bloom from June to September and make good garden plants.

Blazing-star, sand lily, stickleaf

Mentzelia decapetala

The upright, sturdy stems of this native plant, 2 to 4 feet tall, grow in disturbed areas of the western half of the state, increasing westward. The showy white flowers, 3 to 5 inches wide, open about 2 P.M. in sunny weather of August to October and are closed during the night.

Stems are 8 to 20 inches long and may be erect but are usually sprawling. This native plant is found statewide on dry, rocky prairie soils except the far southeastern corner. The small, dull yellow flowers are ½ to ¾ inch wide, open in the mornings, and bloom from June through September.

Stickleaf

Mentzelia oligosperma

Missouri pincushion

Coryphantha missouriensis

Small fat stems, usually in clumps of 3 to 12, stand 2 to 4 inches tall in the eastern half of the state, bearing their greenish to yellowish pink, 2-inch flowers from May to July. This native plant is usually found in dry, rocky prairie soils.

Found in a few sites in the western third of the state, particularly the Panhandle, these vigorous, branching native plants grow 4 to 7 feet tall. The bright magenta to purple flowers are 1½ to 2 inches wide and bloom from May to July (and in gardens nearly statewide).

Walking stick cholla, tree cholla

Cylindropuntia imbricata

Prickly pear

Opuntia engelmannii

This big, 1- to 3-foot-high native cactus is scattered along roadsides and in fencerows in the southern and northwestern sectors of Oklahoma. They prefer rocky habitats and may be upright or nearly prostrate. The upper edges may be covered with 4-inch, yellow to orange flowers during May to July, which are followed by bright red fruits.

Eastern prickly pear
Opuntia humifusa

In pastures, along roadsides, and even in wooded areas statewide, this very common, creeping plant grows only about 1 foot tall. The abundant yellow flowers are often red-centered and 2 to 4 inches across. They bloom from May to July. The fleshy, somewhat pear-shaped fruits of this native plant are edible, with care.

Tall loosestrife, winged loosestrife

Lythrum alatum

Found on mostly wet soils statewide, this native plant has slender, 2- to 4-foot stems that branch near the top. The pink or orchid flowers are usually 6-petaled, ¼ to ½ inch wide, and bloom from May to September. This is not the purple loosestrife that has been declared a noxious weed. It is usually well-behaved.

Meadow-beauty

Rhexia mariana

The more common of our 2 similar species, these 1- to 4-foot-tall plants grow on the always wet soils of ditches, along lake and stream edges, and in bogs in the eastern third of the state. The pink flowers are about 1 inch wide and bloom from June to October. Look for the bright yellow stamens that are bent in the middle.

Sundrops, toothed evening primrose

Oenothera berlandieri

The branched stems of sundrops grow 4 to 20 inches tall on prairie soils of the western two-thirds of Oklahoma, bearing bright bouquets of 1- to 2-inch, yellow 4-petaled flowers in April to August. Unusual for evening primroses, sundrops bloom in the daytime. This plant is native to Oklahoma.

Engelmann's evening primrose

Oenothera engelmannii

These native plants grow 8 to 24 inches tall and are found along open roadsides and on shortgrass prairies of the western quarter of Oklahoma. The white to pink night-blooming flowers are about 1 to 1¼ inches long and bloom from May to August.

Tall gaura, large-flowered gaura

Oenothera longiflora

The branching stems of this native plant rise 2 to 5 feet tall in barrow ditches and along roadsides statewide except in the northwestern corner. The many white to pink flowers, ¾ inch to 1¼ inches long, appear in August to October. Night bloomers, from the roadside they appear to bloom white in the morning and turn pink by afternoon.

Spreading stems 1 to 2 feet long bear 2- to 6-inch white to pink flowers that close at dawn unless the day is very cloudy. These native plants are found on scattered, rocky sandstone or limestone outcrops in the central and southwestern areas in Oklahoma. They bloom from April to July and produce large, 4-winged papery fruits.

Large-flowered evening primrose, Missouri evening primrose

Oenothera macrocarpa

Showy evening primrose

Oenothera speciosa

Found along roadsides and in sunny fields statewide except in the Panhandle, the stems of this native plant are 4 to 20 inches tall, erect or spreading, bearing their day-blooming, 2- to 3-inch white to pink flowers from April to July. Showy evening primroses are weakly perennial but seldom stay in one location for long.

Butler's sandparsley

Ammoselinum butleri

The slender branching stems rise 4 to 15 inches high, bearing deeply dissected, parsley-like leaves and a few tiny white flowers at the branch tips. Growing on damp sandy, granitic, or limestone soils, this native plant is scattered statewide except in the northwestern corner. It blooms from April through May.

Poison hemlock

Conium maculatum

Growing in shallow water or mud statewide except in the Panhandle, this very poisonous, introduced plant blooms from May to August. The hollow branching stems grow 2 to 7 feet tall, with an open, lacy appearance. They are usually mottled with fine purplish specks. The white flowers are individually tiny. This European plant was naturalized during settlement and is similar to the native *Cicuta maculata* (water hemlock).

Plants 2 to 4 feet tall with stiff, branching stems bear striking 1- to 1½-inch heads of small purplish flowers. These native plants are found on sandy or rocky prairies of the eastern two-thirds of Oklahoma and bloom from August to October. They are pleasantly fragrant in bloom.

Rattlesnake master, Leavenworth's eryngo

Eryngium leavenworthii

Button snakeroot, rattlesnake master

Eryngium yuccifolium

The stout, upright stems rise 1 to 4 feet high on rich prairie soils in the eastern two-thirds of Oklahoma. The flower heads are ½ to 1 inch long and produce white to green blooms from May to August.

Another native wetland plant, whorled pennywort is found in the shallow waters of lakes and along river edges in the eastern, south-central, and southwestern areas of the state. The creeping stems are 6 to 16 inches long and bear few-flowered sprays of tiny greenish white flowers from June to October.

Whorled pennywort

Hydrocotyle verticillata

Prairie parsley, prairie parsnip

Polytaenia nuttallii

This large, showy native plant grows 1½ to 4 feet tall on prairies statewide except in the northwestern quarter. Leaves are parsley-like, and masses of yellow flowers appear from April to July, followed by clusters of dry, yellowish seeds.

Smooth, branched stems rise 1 to 3 feet tall in lightly wooded river- and streamside sites in the eastern and south-central areas of the state. This native plant produces yellow blooms from April to July.

Golden alexanders

Zizia aurea

Shooting-star

Dodecatheon meadia

white color variation

These native plants are 1 to 2 feet tall. Long bare stems rise from a leafy base and bear white to rose flowers, 1 inch long, that appear to be folded back from the stamens. The plants are found in the eastern third of Oklahoma, in the south-central portion, and scattered in the southwest, blooming from March to May. The flowers tend to be white in eastern areas and rose-pink westward, but they are all the same species.

Indian pink
Spigelia marilandica

Indian pink is native only to extreme southeastern Oklahoma, where it grows along roads and trails in deeply forested lands. The stems rise 1 to 2 feet tall and each has several red or yellow tubular flowers about 2 inches long and displayed in a whorl of light green leaves. It blooms from May to June. Indian pink is also a popular garden perennial for shaded areas and is often grown around homes.

Mountain pink

Centaurium beyrichii

Mountain pink, a plant native to the state, blooms from June to August on well-drained, rocky and alkaline soils in the south-central and southwestern areas of Oklahoma. Stems only 4 to 7 inches high bear clusters of ⅛-inch, white to pink flowers.

white color variation

The erect stems of this native plant are 10 to 24 inches tall, branched near the top, and have opposite leaves. The blue-violet or, rarely, white flowers are borne in clusters of 2 to 6 and are 2 to 4 inches across. The plant is found in central and western Oklahoma except the Panhandle. Bluebells bloom from June to September on seasonally wet prairie soils.

Prairie bluebells, tulip gentian

Eustoma exaltatum

Prairie rose-gentian, meadow-pink

Sabatia campestris

A common native prairie plant of the eastern two-thirds of Oklahoma, meadow-pink blooms from May to July on sandy prairies, in pastures, and along roadsides. The stems are single and 2 to 9 inches tall, each with a few white to pink flowers, 1 inch wide, at the top.

Unbranched stems rise 8 to 14 inches high from woody roots, bearing clusters of light blue to white flowers that are about ½ inch long and wide. Usually found growing on stony prairie soils, these native plants bloom from March to May in the southern third of Oklahoma.

Fringed blue-star

Amsonia ciliata

Indian hemp, prairie dogbane

Apocynum cannabinum

Found in the entire United States and all over Oklahoma, this sturdy native, roadside weed, stands 1 to 4 feet tall, bearing its small, 1/8-inch white flowers at or near the stem tip. It blooms from May to July. The name Indian hemp comes from its use by Native American tribes as a source of fiber for twine and basketry. Indian hemp contains some highly efficient poisons, and its reputation as a medicinal plant is not reliable.

Antelopehorn

Asclepias asperula

Antelopehorn, a native plant, makes a many-stemmed bouquet that grows in the western three-quarters of Oklahoma but most often in the southern half on sandy or rocky gypsum soils. The plants stand 5 to 25 inches tall, with 1 cluster of up to 36 ¼-inch green flowers at the top of each stem. They bloom from April to July and have a fragrance like lilacs.

Swamp milkweed

Asclepias incarnata

Standing 3 to 9 feet tall, swamp milkweed branches near the top to bear 3 to 12 or more clusters of pretty pink flowers, each about ¼ inch high. This native plant grows in widely scattered locations in marshes, along lakeshores, and in other wet, sunny locations statewide. Occasionally found in bloom as early as July, the plants burst into full glory in September and October.

Butterfly milkweed
Asclepias tuberosa

The most noticeable milkweed in Oklahoma, this native plant is found statewide except in the Panhandle. It is our only milkweed without a milky sap, which may explain why, though its nectar attracts many butterflies, they do not prefer it for laying their eggs. The stems are 1 to 3 feet tall, with many tight clusters of yellow to orange to red flowers, ½ to ¾ inch long, blooming from May to August.

Green-flowered antelopehorn

Asclepias viridiflora

This native plant can be found all over Oklahoma on sandy or rocky prairie soils, blooming from May to August. The stems rise by ones or twos to 4 to 24 inches tall, bearing 1 or more balls of purple-tinged green flowers, ⅓ to ½ inch long, in the upper leaf axils.

Uncommon statewide, twoflower milkweed, a native plant, blooms from April to June. The stems sprawl 4 to 16 inches on poor, often sandy soils of prairies and dunes. The ½-inch purple to violet flowers are borne in pairs along the stems. The plant seems to enjoy the company of sagebrush.

Twoflower milkweed

Matelea biflora

Nuttall's evolvulus

Evolvulus nuttallianus

This is a small, sometimes shrubby plant, 4 to 6 inches tall, that grows in sandy, open locations almost anywhere in Oklahoma, especially on sand dunes. A native, it blooms from April to July, and the flowers, orchid or blue to white, are about ¼ inch long.

Ivy-leaf morning glory

Ipomoea hederacea

These native climbing vines occur mostly as weeds of cultivated land in scattered locations over the body of the state. The blue to violet flowers appear from July to October and are about 1 inch to 2½ inches long. This species hybridizes readily with cultivated morning glories.

Wild sweet-potato

Ipomoea pandurata

Wild sweet-potato is a native twining or trailing vine found in old fields and along roadsides and in fencerows all over the body of the state except the northwestern corner. It blooms from June to September. The flowers are showy, either rose-pink or white with rose centers, and 2 to 3 inches long. There are 7 other species of wild morning glories in the state, some escaped from cultivation.

Standing cypress

Ipomopsis rubra

Usually with just 1 central stem per plant, these spectacular native plants, 3 to 5 feet tall, can be real traffic-stoppers. The red flowers are clustered at the top and have inch-long tubes with corollas spread about ½ inch wide. The leaves are deeply divided, fernlike, and whorled around the stem. Found on sunny, gravelly soils in the central, southeastern, and southwestern areas of the state, the plants bloom from May to October.

Sweet William, blue phlox

Phlox divaricata

Sweet William can be found in the leaf litter of open woods and on rocky hills of the eastern third of Oklahoma. The plants reach 6 to 12 inches tall and spread about as wide. The flowers are ½ to ¾ inch long and wide, blooming from March to May. Sweet William is native to Oklahoma.

Jacob's ladder blooms on low spreading stems, 6 to 20 inches long, in damp woods in the eastern quarter of the state, with one collection having been made in the Panhandle. As it is a popular shade-garden plant, it might be found anywhere the right conditions exist. The blue flowers are ¼ to ½ inch long and wide and bloom in April and May. This is Oklahoma's only native species of *Polemonium*.

Jacob's ladder, creeping polemonium

Polemonium reptans

Hairy blue curls

Phacelia hirsuta

These densely hairy native plants grow 4 to 20 inches high on sandy soils at forest edges in the eastern two-thirds of Oklahoma. The showy blue flowers are about ½ inch wide and are borne in small clusters from April to May. The fruits are dry, papery capsules with several dry seeds inside. Look for them along country roads, where they often grow in abundance.

Stems of pretty puccoon grow 3 to 16 inches tall and bear small clusters of relatively large, yellow, frilled-petal flowers in March to June. They are often seen in developed areas, where the plant blooms beside curbs and sidewalks in all areas of the state. But they are true native wildflowers and grow as well in dry, sandy or rocky pastures and forest openings. The flowers are ½ inch to 2 inches long, with bells ¾ to 1 inch wide.

Pretty puccoon

Lithospermum incisum

Marbleseed

Onosmodium molle

Marbleseed forms clumps 20 to 40 inches tall, with flowers bell-shaped, ¼ to ½ inch long, and never wide open. The variety illustrated, *occidentalis*, grows on dry, sandy or gravelly prairies, but the variety *molle* can be found in eastern Oklahoma in forest openings. Marbleseed produces white to green blooms in May and June in widely scattered locations across the state.

Sand verbena, rose vervain

Glandularia canadensis

One of the earliest wildflowers to bloom, this native plant strongly resembles the perennial verbenas of garden shops. Look for it in March, occasionally until June, at the edges of forests, in pastures and fencerows, and along roadsides, usually on sandy soil, and statewide except for the northwestern corner. The flowers are pink to orchid.

Fogfruit, frog fruit

Phyla nodiflora

These native plants are prostrate or ascending on stems 1 to 3 feet long and bear the little ½-inch pink or white rosettes of typical verbena-style flowers on thin pedicels 2 to 3 inches long. Usually found in damp sunny locations, they bloom from April to September in scattered sites all over the body of the state.

Stems are erect, 8 to 50 inches tall, with narrow spikes bearing deep blue or purple flowers about ½ inch wide. Hoary vervain is native to Oklahoma and common across the entire state along roadsides, in pastures, and in old fields. It blooms from May to August.

Hoary vervain, wooly vervain

Verbena stricta

Dittany, wild oregano

Cunila origanoides

Dittany's arching stems grow 1 to 2 feet long. The orchid or pink flowers are few to 27 in a cluster and ¼ to ½ inch long. This native plant blooms from August to November on damp, rocky forest margins and along streams in the eastern one-fourth of Oklahoma. It is not a common wildflower but one worth looking for. It keeps good company.

Lemon beebalm blooms from May to July on sandy or rocky prairies in all parts of Oklahoma. Because this native plant is a popular choice for roadside plantings, it is often seen along highways. The plants are 12 to 30 inches tall, with the flowers in separate clusters around the upper stems. The flowers are about ½ to ¾ inch long, predominantly orchid in color, with pale or purplish bracts beneath. The entire plant is lemon-scented.

Lemon monarda, lemon beebalm

Monarda citriodora

color variation

Virginia mountain mint

Pycnanthemum virginianum

Mountain mints grow 16 to 40 inches high and bloom from July to September in prairie potholes, wet woodlands, and meadows in scattered locations over central Oklahoma. The white flowers are ⅛ to ¾ inch long, and are clustered at the top of leafy stems. Virginia mountain mint is native to Oklahoma.

Plants are 20 to 60 inches tall, with straight, mostly unbranched stems. This native plant prefers the dry, sandy or rocky soils of prairies and roadsides. The fall-blooming flowers are arranged in loose spikes along the upper stems and are ½ to 1 inch long and pale blue to deep blue. They grow in all parts of Oklahoma and are often seen associated with Indiangrass.

Blue sage, Pitcher's sage

Salvia azurea

Clammy ground cherry, husk-tomato

Physalis heterophylla

Bell-shaped yellow flowers about ¾ inch long and wide hang under the upper leaves on plants 8 to 16 inches tall. Each flower has a center smudged with grayish brown. The stems are fairly weak, making the plants somewhat spreading. The ripe fruit of ground cherries is edible; and pioneer women made them into jams, while the Plains Indians ate them raw or cooked with chilis for a sauce. The green fruit is often poisonous in varying degrees. Ground cherries are found over most of Oklahoma except the far northwest. *Physalis* fruits are surrounded by papery husks (Chinese lanterns).

Silverleaf nightshade

Solanum elaeagnifolium

Pretty enough to be grown in a garden, the native silverleaf nightshade grows wild in disturbed sites in western and southwestern Oklahoma. The flowers are ¾ inch to 1½ inches across and are usually an attractive dark blue. Blooms appear from May to August, followed by yellow tomato-like fruits, which are not to be eaten. The leaves bear a distinctive covering of silvery scalelike hairs on the underside. The spreading stems are spineless and 10 to 40 inches tall. The fruit of a wild *Solanum* should not be eaten.

Prairie beardtongue, prairie penstemon, false foxglove

Penstemon cobaea

Prairie beardtongue is common during May in the whole body of Oklahoma except the extreme eastern counties and the Panhandle. This native plant will bloom occasionally from April to July if the weather is mild. The inset shows the purple form, a more southern variety found near U.S. 70 as it crosses southern Oklahoma just north of the Red River. On stiffly upright stems 8 to 28 inches high, the big 2-inch white to pink, purple, or orchid flowers form loose spikes. The wide-open throats are a perfect fit for the bodies of our largest bumblebees.

Our very own penstemon grows wild only in Oklahoma, along the border between the crosstimbers and the prairies. Narrow, inch-long white or pale yellow flowers are clustered on stems 14 to 24 inches long. Some of our other penstemons also have white flowers, but this is the only one that keeps its mouth shut, with the lower lip firmly pressed against the upper. It likes sun, sandy or loamy soils, and good drainage.

Oklahoma penstemon

Penstemon oklahomensis

Yellow gerardia

Aureolaria grandiflora

Uncommon in forested areas of the far eastern and southeastern counties, this great yellow flower will get your attention with loose clusters of blooms about 2 inches long on stems that may reach 3 to 5 feet tall. It is a fall bloomer, appearing from late July into October, and prefers well-watered sites.

Red Indian paintbrush

Castilleja indivisa

Any open space in the southern two-thirds of the state where the grass isn't too dense and with plenty of water is a fine place for this native annual paintbrush to appear, though more commonly toward the east. In dry years it blooms in April, in wet years from April to July. The inset photograph shows one of the many color variations of *Castilleja purpurea*, or prairie paintbrush, which is common in northern and southwestern Oklahoma.

prairie paintbrush

Common lousewort, red fern, yellow betony

Pedicularis canadensis

This plant is the "red fern" of the old children's book, named for its fern-like leaves, which are reddish when they emerge in the spring. By bloom time, April and May, the leaves are grass green and the yellow pinwheel of inch-long flowers on stems 4 to 12 inches tall shows it not to be a fern at all. Look for it anywhere in the eastern one-fourth of the state.

Often found in part shade, this native plant prefers the dry sandy soils of the eastern three-fourths of the state, blooming from May to August—but only in the morning. With full sun, the flowers close for the day. The showy flowers are purple or lavender and 1½ to 3 inches across.

Wild petunia
Ruellia humilis

Prairie bluet, star-violet

Houstonia nigricans

Prairie bluet likes dry, rocky sites, where it attains a height of 5 to 20 inches and blooms from May to September anywhere in Oklahoma, though more commonly in the west. Of note is the fine furry pelt on the little petals. Each of the many little white-pink-blue flowers is less than ¼ inch wide. Prairie bluet is native to Oklahoma.

Red honeysuckle, trumpet honeysuckle

Lonicera sempervirens

This beautiful, native evergreen flowering vine makes thickety tangles in creek- and lakeside habitats all over the central and eastern parts of the state, but especially in the Red River bottoms of the southeast. The vines climb to 20 feet or more, bearing masses of red, yellow-tipped flowers about 2 inches long. The flowers attract hummingbirds, and the long blooming period, with a flush in the spring and scattered flowers all summer and fall, keep them well fed. In the autumn, the small shining red berries are a favorite food of bluebirds, robins, and mockingbirds.

Coyote gourd, railroad vine, buffalo gourd

Cucurbita foetidissima

Called by many names, this native species makes conspicuous vines 6 to 20 feet long in fencerows and other waste places. The big yellow flowers are 3 to 4 inches long and wide, nestled among the large rough leaves. The plant bears greenish gourds with thin shells that are smooth, striped, and 2 to 4 inches long. It is found in all parts of the state, though most often in the western half, and blooms in the mornings of May to July.

Creeping cucumber, melonette

Melothria pendula

Creeping cucumber would be a most modest little plant if it were not so widespread and persistent. This native plant is found in most of Oklahoma with the exception of the far northwest. The smooth, slender vines climb on fences and roadside plants to hang their edible 1-inch green melons. The yellow flowers are about ¼ inch long.

Cardinal flower

Lobelia cardinalis

This species has been found in every part of the state, often in streambeds and always in very moist ground. The 1- to 2-inch blood-red flowers are clustered at the top of stems 1 to 4 feet tall, and show well against the deep colors of fall. The plant blooms from August to November. It is native to Oklahoma.

Great blue lobelia

Lobelia siphilitica

This beautiful native plant grows in seeps and other shallow water in the eastern half of the state. The bright blue to violet flowers top spikes ½ to 3 feet tall and bloom from July to October in the southeastern and south-central parts of the state.

Yarrow

Achillea millefolium

Yarrow is found all over the Northern Hemisphere and has been used as an herbal medicine since ancient times. Most bloom in May, when they spread their pretty white to pink flowers in lawns, vacant lots, along roadsides, and in fields until the heat of July arrives. You must get close to see that the individual flowers are indeed built on the sunflower plan, with a central disk of tubular flowers surrounded by tiny white petal-like rays. The plants range from 8 to 20 inches tall, with the tiny flower heads massed into 2- to 3-inch clusters. Only 1 species of *Achillea* is recognized; the colorful garden varieties have been created by gardeners from chance mutations.

Pussytoes

Antennaria parlinii

One of the first flowers to bloom in the spring, this dainty woodland flower appears in March and April. The little white to pink florets are clustered in small rounded clumps similar to a kitten's paw; hence its common name. There are 3 species of *Antennaria* in Oklahoma, of which this is the most common, appearing in the eastern three-quarters of the state.

Doze daisy, lazy daisy

Aphanostephus skirrhobasis

This bright white to lavender daisy begins to show in May and will continue right through the summer. The heads are 1 to 2 inches broad. As in chrysanthemums, the rays are purplish on the underside. But it waits for the sun to become warm before unrolling for each day's work, earning its common name for its late-sleeping habit. This native plant is most common in open sunny areas, especially on the plains of western Oklahoma, and is often associated with lemon monarda and Indian blanket.

Basket flower, a native species, blooms over much of the central part of the state, but in widely scattered communities. It is in bloom from late May to early July, with a peak in June. The bristly bracts below the white or pink florets are fringelike, weaving themselves into a fair semblance of a basket holding the pale pink-and-white threadlike flowers. They like damp soils and are often found at the base of hills, in barrow ditches, and in wet meadows. The plants are 3 to 7 feet tall and showy, with single heads 3 to 4 inches wide.

American basket flower

Centaurea americana

Tickseed, lance-leaf tickseed

Coreopsis lanceolata

In central, eastern, and southern Oklahoma, tickseed grows on well-drained soils, especially sandy or rocky areas, from April to June, with a peak in May. The plants grow 20 to 60 inches tall, usually about 24 inches, and hold their flowers high on leafless branches. The flower heads are 2 to 3 inches across. This species is the perennial coreopsis that Bess Snodgrass planted all over the Oklahoma Arbuckles area, where it has naturalized; the inset photo shows *Coreopsis tinctoria*, plains coreopsis, an annual.

plains coreopsis

This native plant may be found in any part of Oklahoma but is most common in the western two-thirds of the state. It blooms from late May through July. The attractive flowers, 3 to 4 inches wide, have a stiff brownish center surrounded by pink to magenta rays. The plant prefers dry prairie soils. Oklahoma has 6 species of *Echinacea*, 2 of which, *Echinacea pallida* or pale coneflower and *Echinacea purpurea*, or purple coneflower (which is also yellow to green), are shown in the inset photos.

Narrow-leaf coneflower

Echinacea angustifolia

purple coneflower

pale coneflower

Elephant's foot

Elephantopus carolinianus

Elephant's foot, a native species, blooms in moist shady habitats all over the state except the Panhandle. Blooming spans July through October, with a peak in September. The plants are well branched and 1 to 3 feet tall, with white to lavender or blue flowers borne at the branch tips. The 3 green bracts below the flower head are said to resemble an elephant's footprint.

Daisy fleabane

Erigeron strigosus

Blooming from May to July, with a peak in June, this native plant is found in the entire state except the Panhandle, on any soil, in open sunny sites. It is common along roadsides, where plants form a bright white background for more colorful wildflowers. The stems are usually 1½ to 2½ feet tall, with many half-inch white daisies with a yellow center.

Boneset, tall thoroughwort

Eupatorium altissimum

Bonesets bloom from August to October in central and southeastern Oklahoma, along ditches, pond margins, and in marshes. They require sun and moist soils. These native plants grow 3 to 4 feet tall, with white flower clusters 2 to 4 inches across. Oklahoma has 12 species of *Eupatorium*, all with white, blue, or pink flowers; *Eupatorium purpureum*, sweetscented joe pye weed, is shown in the inset photo.

sweetscented joe pye weed

Indian blanket, firewheels

Gaillardia pulchella

The many common names for this native species acknowledge the attractive nature of this winter annual. It is the official Oklahoma state wildflower. Indian blankets bloom from April to August, with a peak in May, and are more common in western and central Oklahoma. This is a prairie plant, preferring full sun and perfect drainage. The plants range from 6 inches to more than 12 inches tall, and the flowering heads span 1½ to 2½ inches. Although most have yellow tips on red rays, some are all red, and a few are red-yellow-white. *Gaillardia aestivalis*, summer gaillardia (see inset photo), is all yellow.

summer gaillardia

Maximilian's sunflower

Helianthus maximiliani

These native sunflowers brighten sunny roadsides anywhere in the state but are most common in the central areas. The perennial plants emerge in spring and grow 2 to 3 feet tall, often with one bright yellow flower at the tip that never quite opens. Then, in a rush after the heat of summer, they zoom to 5 to 8 feet tall, with the new growth a riot of bright, all-yellow sunflowers, 2 to 4 inches wide. October is their peak month.

Ragworts bloom from April to May, along sunny roadsides and in waste places over the entire state. This native species is one of the first yellow composites to bloom (except for dandelions, which bloom all year long). The plants are 8 to 24 inches tall and bear flower heads that are about ½ to 1 inch across in clusters of 6 to 20.

Prairie ragwort

Packera plattensis

Sand palafox

Palafoxia sphacelata

Look for palafox in dunes and along sandy roadsides from June to October in the western half of Oklahoma. The individual pink flower heads are less than 1 inch wide and usually appear in small clusters on plants 8 to 16 inches tall. These native plants are often found on sandy soils. There are 2 other species of *Palafoxia* in Oklahoma, but they are less common and have no ray florets and so are less conspicuous.

Compass plant

Silphium laciniatum

This is the plant claimed by Aldo Leopold to be the signature plant of the tallgrass prairie. It blooms from May to August in the entire body of Oklahoma but has not been found in the Panhandle. Unfortunately, cattle eat this native plant to the ground, so it is usually not found inside fenced areas. The upright stems, 3 to 6 feet tall, bear spikes of 2½- to 3½-inch yellow heads that are slightly sticky to the touch. The compass function refers to the north-south orientation of the huge basal leaves.

Goat's beard

Tragopogon dubius

Goat's beard can be found over the entire state except the southeastern corner between April and October, with a peak in June. The flowering heads of this native plant are conspicuous enough, but exceeded by the prominent green bracts. The seed heads are huge, 4 inches across. Goat's beard prefers prairie soils and the openings provided by roads and paths.

seed head

Glossary

ACHENE A small, hard fruit with a single seed that is fused to the cell wall. For example, the "seeds" of a strawberry are achenes.

ALTERNATE The positioning of leaves on a stem in a one-at-a-node pattern. This is the more common arrangement on broadleaf plants and on grasses and lilies. See also Opposite.

BINOMIAL The system of naming species of living things that was invented by Carl Linnaeus. It consists of a generic name, establishing a relationship, and a specific epithet. For example, in the name *Sagittaria latifolia*, *Sagittaria* is the generic name and *latifolia* is the species name. See also Genus.

BRACTS Specialized leaves that are part of the flowering section of a plant. Usually they are leaflike in texture but are smaller and positioned directly under the flower.

CANE A hard, jointed aerial stem in grasses, or a perennial stem from a perennial base, as in blackberries.

CAPSULES Fruits that are dry and papery, with dry seeds inside.

DISK FLOWERS Small tubular flowers that are tightly packed into the center of most composites.

FRUIT The mature ovary after fertilization, with any other structures remaining with it. Some examples are the capsule of a penstemon, and the small dry seed of a grass.

GENUS The taxonomic group that is immediately above species; the first part of a binomial name (see also Binomial). The plural of genus is genera.

HERB A plant with no woody parts aboveground.

INFLORESCENCE Parts of a flowering plant to which the flowers or fruits are attached.

OPPOSITE Positioning of leaves on a stem in a two-at-a-node pattern (see also Alternate).

PANICLE An inflorescence that is much-branched, with the ultimate flowers remote from the main axis.

RAY FLOWERS Specialized outer flowers arranged around the outside of a disk in composites. These usually resemble the petals on a simple flower.

RECURVED Gradually bent or turned backward.

SPADIX A spike with a fleshy axis, bearing small, close-set flowers.

SPECIES The second word of a binomial name, designating a specific kind of plant or animal. Plants of a species usually share similar habitat and form, and can interbreed.

SPIKE Inflorescence with a central stem and one or more closely attached flowers.

SUCCULENT Firm and fleshy or juicy.

Bibliography

Correll, D. S., and M. C. Johnston. 1970. *Manual of the vascular plants of Texas*. Renner, Tex.: Texas Research Foundation.

Flora of North America Editorial Committee. 1993–2005. *Flora of North America*. Vols. 1–5, 23–26. New York: Oxford University Press.

Goodman, George. 1958. *Spring flora of Oklahoma*. Norman, Okla.: University of Oklahoma Duplicating Service.

Great Plains Flora Association. 1986. *Flora of the Great Plains*. Lawrence, Kan.: University Press of Kansas.

Kindscher, Kelly. 1987. *Edible wild plants of the prairie: An ethnobotanical guide*. Lawrence, Kan.: University Press of Kansas.

Ladd, Doug, and Frank Oberle. 1995. *Tallgrass prairie wildflowers: A field guide*. Guilford, Conn.: Globe Pequot Press.

McCoy, Doyle. 1976. *Roadside wildflowers of Oklahoma*. 2 vols. Self-published.

Oklahoma Biological Survey. 2005. *Vascular plants database*. Norman, Okla.: University of Oklahoma. http://www.geo.ou.edu/botanical/.

Taylor, R. J., and C. E. S. Taylor. 1994. *An annotated list of the ferns, fern allies, gymnosperms and flowering plants of Oklahoma*. 3d ed. Durant, Okla.: Self-published.

Tyrl, R. J., S. C. Barber, P. Buck, J. R. Estes, P. Folley, L. K. Magrath, C. Murray, A. Ryburn, B. Smith, C. E. S. Taylor,

R. A. Thompson, W. Elisens, C. Murray, J. Walker, and L. Watson. 2010. *Keys and descriptions for the vascular plants of Oklahoma*. Noble, Okla.: Flora of Oklahoma, Inc.

Tyrl, R., T. Bidwell, and R. Masters. 2002. *Field guide to Oklahoma plants*. Stillwater, Okla.: Oklahoma State University, Department of Plant and Soil Sciences.

U.S. Department of Agriculture, Natural Resources Conservation Service. 2011. *The PLANTS database*. Baton Rouge, La.: National Plant Data Center. http://www.plants.usda.gov.

Yatskievych, G. 1999. *Steyermark's flora of Missouri*. Rev. ed., vol. 1. St. Louis, Mo.: Missouri Botanical Garden.

Name Index

acacia, prairie, 91
Acacia angustissima, 91
Acanthaceae, 13
acanthus family, 13
Achillea millefolium, 202
alexanders, golden, 159
Alismataceae, 1
Allium canadense, 35
amaryllis family, 3
Ammoselinum butleri, 153
Amorpha canescens, 98
Amsonia ciliata, 165
Andropogon gerardii, 18
Androstephium coeruleum, 36
anemone, Carolina, 63
anemone, prairie, 63
anemone, rue, 64
Anemone caroliniana, 63
Anemonella thalictroides, 64
antelopehorn, 167
antelopehorn, green-flowered, 170
Antennaria parlinii, 203
Aphanostephus skirrhobasis, 204
Apiaceae, 10
Apios americana, 99
Apocynaceae, 11
Apocynum cannabinum, 166
Aquilegia canadensis, 65
Araceae, 2
Argemone polyanthemos, 70

Arisaema dracontium, 28
arrowhead, broadleaf, 17
arum family, 2
Asclepias asperula, 167
Asclepias incarnata, 168
Asclepias tuberosa, 169
Asclepias viridiflora, 170
Asteraceae, 14
Astragalus missouriensis, 100
Aureolaria grandiflora, 192
avens, white, 87

Baptisia australis, 101
Baptisia sphaerocarpa, 101
basket flower, American, 205
bean, amberique, 112
bean, wild, 112
bean family, 6
beardtongue, prairie, 190
beebalm, lemon, 185
beeplant, Rocky Mountain, 82
bellflower family, 14
betony, yellow, 194
bladderpod, 106
bladderpod, spreading, 80
blazing-star, 140
bloodroot, 71
blue bell, 66
bluebells, prairie, 163
blue curls, hairy, 178

blue-star, fringed, 165
bluestem, big, 18
bluestem, little, 22
bluet, prairie, 196
bog-iris, 43
boneset, 210
borage family, 11–12
Boraginaceae, 11–12
Bouteloua curtipendula, 19
Brassicaceae, 5
briar, sensitive, 93
broomrape family, 13
Buchloe dactyloides, 20
buckwheat, annual, 52
buckwheat family, 4
bull-nettle, 127
bulrush, great, 26
bulrush, hardstem, 26
bundleflower, Illinois, 92
buttercup, early, 68
buttercup, prairie, 68
buttercup family, 5

Cactaceae, 9
cactus family, 9
Caesalpinia jamesii, 95
Callirhoe involucrata, 131
Calopogon oklahomensis, 46
camass, eastern, 37
Camassia scilloides, 37
Campanulaceae, 14
caper family, 6
Capparaceae, 6
Caprifoliaceae, 13
Capsella bursa-pastoris, 75
Cardamine concatenata, 76
cardinal flower, 200
Carex lupulina, 24
carrot family, 10
Caryophyllaceae, 4
Castilleja indivisa, 193
Castilleja purpurea, 193
catclaw, 93
Centaurea americana, 205
Centaurium beyrichii, 162
Cerastium glomeratum, 58
Chamaecrista fasciculata, 96
Chamaesyce maculata, 126

chatterbox, 48
chickweed, clammy, 58
chickweed, common, 61
cholla, tree, 143
cholla, walking stick, 143
Cicuta maculata, 154
cinquefoil, old-field, 88
clammyweed, roughseed, 83
Claytonia virginica, 56
clematis, Pitcher's, 66
Clematis pitcheri, 66
Cleome serrulata, 82
Clitoria mariana, 102
cloth-of-gold, 80
clover, bush, 108
clover, golden prairie, 103
clover, purple prairie, 104
clover, white, 114
clover, yellow sweet-, 109
Cnidoscolus texanus, 127
coffee family, 13
columbine, red, 65
columbine, wild, 65
Commelinaceae, 2
Commelina erecta, 30
compass plant, 215
coneflower, narrow-leaf, 207
coneflower, pale, 207
coneflower, purple, 207
Conium maculatum, 154
Convolvulaceae, 11
coreopsis, plains, 206
Coreopsis lanceolata, 206
Coreopsis tinctoria, 206
corydalis, golden, 72
corydalis, mealy, 73
Corydalis aurea, 72
Corydalis crystallina, 73
Coryphantha missouriensis, 142
cranesbill, 113
Crassulaceae, 6
crazyweed, 110
croton, wooly, 128
Croton capitatus, 128
crow-poison, 41
cucumber, creeping, 199
Cucurbitaceae, 13–14
Cucurbita foetidissima, 198

Cunila origanoides, 184
Cylindropuntia imbricata, 143
Cyperaceae, 2
cypress, standing, 175
Cypripedium kentuckiense, 47

daisy, doze, 204
daisy, lazy, 204
Dalea aurea, 103
Dalea purpurea, 104
dayflower, slender, 30
dayflower family, 2
Desmanthus illinoensis, 92
Desmodium glutinosum, 105
dewberry, southern, 90
Dicentra cucullaria, 74
Dimorphocarpa candicans, 77
dittany, 184
dock, pale, 54
dock, tall, 54
Dodecatheon meadia, 160
dogbane, prairie, 166
dogbane family, 11
dragon, green, 28
dragonroot, 28
Dutchman's breeches, 74

Echinacea angustifolia, 207
Echinacea pallida, 207
Echinacea purpurea, 207
Eleocharis montevidensis, 25
Elephantopus carolinianus, 208
elephant's foot, 208
Epipactis gigantea, 48
Erigeron strigosus, 209
Eriogonum annuum, 52
Erodium cicutarium, 117
Eryngium leavenworthii, 155
Eryngium yuccifolium, 156
eryngo, Leavenworth's, 155
Erysimum asperum, 78
Erythronium albidum, 38
Eupatorium altissimum, 210
Eupatorium purpureum, 210
Euphorbiaceae, 8
Euphorbia marginata, 129
Eustoma exaltatum, 163
evening primrose, Engelmann's, 149
evening primrose, large-flowered, 151
evening primrose, Missouri, 151
evening primrose, showy, 152
evening primrose, toothed, 148
evening primrose family, 10
evolvulus, Nuttall's, 172
Evolvulus nuttallianus, 172

Fabaceae, 6
filaria, 117
fire-pink, 60
firewheels, 211
five finger, 88
flag, southern blue, 43
flame flower, 57
flax, blue, 121
flax, grooved, 123
flax, prairie, 121, 122
flax, stiffstem, 122
flax family, 7
fleabane, daisy, 209
flower-of-an-hour, 57
fogfruit, 182
four o'clock, smooth, 55
four o'clock family, 4
foxglove, false, 190
Fragaria virginiana, 86
frog fruit, 182
Fumariaceae, 5
fumitory family, 5

gaillardia, summer, 211
Gaillardia aestivalis, 211
Gaillardia pulchella, 211
garlic, false, 41
garlic, wild, 35
gaura, large-flowered, 150
gaura, tall, 150
gentian, prairie rose-, 164
gentian, tulip, 163
Gentianaceae, 10–11
gentian family, 10–11
Geraniaceae, 7
Geranium carolinianum, 118
geranium family, 7
gerardia, yellow, 192
Geum canadense, 87
glade-cress, golden, 79

Glandularia canadensis, 181
goat's beard, 216
goat's rue, 113
gourd, buffalo, 198
gourd, coyote, 198
gourd family, 13–14
grama, sideoats, 19
grass, blue-eyed, 45
grass, buffalo, 20
grass family, 1
grass-pink, Oklahoma, 46
ground cherry, clammy, 188
ground nut, American, 99

Helianthus maximiliani, 212
hemlock, poison, 154
hemlock, water, 154
hemp, Indian, 166
hogwort, 128
honeysuckle, red, 197
honeysuckle, trumpet, 197
honeysuckle family, 13
Houstonia nigricans, 196
husk-tomato, 188
hyacinth, water, 32
hyacinth, wild, 37
Hybanthus verticillatus, 135
Hydrocotyle verticillata, 157
Hydrophyllaceae, 11
Hymenocallis caroliniana, 39
Hypericaceae, 8
Hypericum drummondii, 133
Hypericum perforatum, 134
Hypoxis hirsuta, 40

Indian blanket, 211
Indiangrass, 23
indigo, southern, 101
indigo, western, 107
indigo, wild blue, 101
indigo, yellow wild, 101
Indigofera miniata, 107
Ipomoea hederacea, 173
Ipomoea pandurata, 174
Ipomopsis rubra, 175
Iridaceae, 3
iris, prairie, 44
iris family, 3

Iris virginica, 43

Jacob's ladder, 177
jewelweed, 81
joe pye weed, sweetscented, 210
Johnny-jump-up, 136
Juncaceae, 3
Juncus marginatus, 33

Klamath weed, 134
Krameriaceae, 7
Krameria lanceolata, 116

ladies' tress, Great Plains, 50
lady's slipper, yellow, 47
Lamiaceae, 12
leadplant, 98
leather flower, 66
Leavenworthia aurea, 79
legume family, 6
lespedeza, roundhead, 108
Lespedeza capitata, 108
Lesquerella gracilis, 80
Liliaceae, 3
lily, celestial, 44
lily, funnel, 36
lily, sand, 140
lily, summer spider, 39
lily, white trout, 38
lily family, 3
Linaceae, 7
linen family, 7
Linum pratense, 121
Linum rigidum, 122
Linum sulcatum, 123
Linum usitatissimum, 7
Lithospermum incisum, 179
Loasaceae, 9
lobelia, great blue, 201
Lobelia cardinalis, 200
Lobelia siphilitica, 201
locoweed, purple, 110
Loganiaceae, 10
logania family, 10
Lonicera sempervirens, 197
loosestrife, tall, 146
loosestrife, winged, 146
loosestrife family, 9

lotus, American, 62
lotus family, 5
lousewort, common, 194
Lupinus species, 111
Luzula bulbosa, 34
Lythraceae, 9
Lythrum alatum, 146

mallow, purple poppy, 131
mallow, scarlet globe, 132
mallow family, 8
Malvaceae, 8
marbleseed, 180
Matelea biflora, 171
May-pop, 139
meadow-beauty, 147
meadow-beauty family, 9
meadow-pink, 164
meadow rue, purple, 69
Melastomaceae, 9
melilot, yellow, 109
Melilotus officinalis, 109
melonette, 199
Melothria pendula, 199
Mentzelia decapetala, 140
Mentzelia oligosperma, 141
milkvetch, Missouri, 100
milkweed, butterfly, 169
milkweed, swamp, 168
milkweed, twoflower, 171
milkweed family, 11
milkwort, bitter, 125
milkwort, pink, 125
milkwort, slender, 125
milkwort, white, 124
milkwort, whorled, 124
milkwort family, 7
Mimosa quadrivalvis, 93
mint family, 12
Minuartia drummondii, 59
Mirabilis glabra, 55
monarda, lemon, 185
Monarda citriodora, 185
morning glory, ivy-leaf, 173
morning glory family, 11
mountain mint, Virginia, 186
mustard family, 5

Nelumbo lutea, 62
Nelumbonaceae, 5
Nemastylis geminiflora, 44
neptunia, 94
Neptunia lutea, 94
nightshade, silverleaf, 189
nightshade family, 12
nits-and-lice, 133
noseburn, 130
Nothoscordum bivalve, 41
nutrush, fringed, 27
Nyctaginaceae, 4

Oenothera berlandieri, 148
Oenothera engelmannii, 149
Oenothera longiflora, 150
Oenothera macrocarpa, 151
Oenothera speciosa, 152
Onagraceae, 10
onion, wild, 35
Onosmodium molle, 180
Opuntia engelmannii, 144
Opuntia humifusa, 145
orchid, three-birds, 51
orchid, yellow fringed, 49
Orchidaceae, 4
orchid family, 4
oregano, wild, 184
Orobanchaceae, 13
Oxalidaceae, 7
Oxalis stricta, 119
Oxalis violacea, 120
Oxytropis lambertii, 110

Packera plattensis, 213
paintbrush, prairie, 193
paintbrush, red Indian, 193
palafox, sand, 214
Palafoxia sphacelata, 214
Panicum virgatum, 21
pansy, field, 136
Papaveraceae, 5
parsley, prairie, 158
parsnip, prairie, 158
Passifloraceae, 9
Passiflora incarnata, 139
passion flower, 139
passion flower family, 9

pea, butterfly, 102
pea, partridge, 96
pea, scarlet, 107
Pedicularis canadensis, 194
Pediomelum cuspidatum, 111
pennywort, whorled, 157
penstemon, Oklahoma, 191
penstemon, prairie, 190
Penstemon cobaea, 190
Penstemon oklahomensis, 191
petunia, wild, 195
Phacelia hirsuta, 178
phlox, blue, 176
Phlox divaricata, 176
phlox family, 11
Phyla nodiflora, 182
Physalis heterophylla, 188
pickerelweed, 32
pickerelweed family, 3
pigeon's wings, 102
pincushion, Missouri, 142
pink, Indian, 161
pink, mountain, 162
pink, rock-, 57
pink family, 4
pink family, Indian, 10
pinkweed, 53
Plantaginaceae, 12
plantain family, 12
Platanthera ciliaris, 49
Poaceae, 1
pogonia, nodding, 51
Polanisia dodecandra, 83
Polemoniaceae, 11
polemonium, creeping, 177
Polemonium reptans, 177
Polygala alba, 124
Polygalaceae, 7
Polygala incarnata, 125
Polygala polygama, 125
Polygala verticillata, 124
Polygonaceae, 7
Polygonum pensylvanicum, 53
Polytaenia nuttallii, 158
Pontederiaceae, 3
Pontederia cordata, 32
poppy, prickly, 70
poppy family, 5

Portulacaceae, 4
potato, duck, 17
potato, wild sweet-, 174
Potentilla simplex, 88
prickly pear, 144
prickly pear, eastern, 145
primrose family, 10
Primulaceae, 10
puccoon, pretty, 179
puff, yellow, 94
purslane family, 4
pussytoes, 203
Pycnanthemum virginianum, 186

ragwort, prairie, 213
railroad vine, 198
Ranunculaceae, 5
Ranunculus aquatilis, 67
Ranunculus fascicularis, 68
ratany, trailing, 116
ratany family, 7
rattlesnake master, 155, 156
red fern, 194
redroot, 87
Rhexia mariana, 147
Rosa carolina, 89
Rosaceae, 6
Rosa multiflora, 89
rose, multiflora, 89
rose, pasture, 89
rose family, 6
Rubiaceae, 13
Rubus trivialis, 90
Ruellia humilis, 195
Rumex altissimus, 54
rush, grassleaf, 33
rush family, 3
rush-pea, James', 95

Sabatia campestris, 164
sage, blue, 187
sage, Pitcher's, 187
Sagittaria latifolia, 17
Salvia azurea, 187
sandparsley, Butler's, 153
sandwort, Drummond's, 59
Sanguinaria canadensis, 71
Schizachyrium scoparium, 22

Schoenoplectus acutus, 26
Schrankia nuttallii, 93
Scleria ciliata, 27
scrambled eggs, 72
scurf-pea, tallbread, 111
sedge, hop, 24
sedge family, 2
Sedum nuttallianum, 84
Sedum pulchellum, 85
senna, wild, 97
Senna marilandica, 97
Sesbania vesicaria, 106
sheep sour, 119
shepherd's purse, 75
shooting-star, 160
Silene virginica, 60
silktop, 103
Silphium laciniatum, 215
Sisyrinchium angustifolium, 45
smartweed, Pennsylvania, 53
snakeroot, button, 156
snow-on-the-mountain, 129
Solanaceae, 12
Solanum elaeagnifolium, 189
Sorghastrum nutans, 23
spectacle-pod, 77
Sphaeralcea coccinea, 132
spiderwort, Ohio, 31
Spigelia marilandica, 161
spikerush, sand, 25
Spiranthes magnicamporum, 50
spring beauty, 56
spurge, prostrate milk, 126
spurge, spotted, 126
spurge family, 8
stargrass, yellow, 40
Stellaria media, 61
stickleaf, 9, 140, 141
stickleaf family, 9
St. John's-wort, common, 134
St. John's-wort family, 8
stonecrop, pink, 85
stonecrop, yellow, 84
stonecrop family, 6
stork's bill, 117
strawberry, wild, 86
Streptanthus hyacinthoides, 81
Strophostyles helvola, 112

sundrops, 148
sunflower, Maximilian's, 212
sunflower family, 14
sweet William, 176
switchgrass, 21

Talinum calycinum, 57
ten-petal, 61
Tephrosia virginiana, 113
Thalictrum dasycarpum, 69
thoroughwort, tall, 210
tickclover, large-flowered, 105
tickclover, sticky, 105
tickseed, 206
tickseed, lance-leaf, 206
tomato family, 12
toothcup, 76
toothwort, 76
Tradescantia ohiensis, 31
Tragia ramosa, 130
Tragopogon dubius, 216
Trifolium repens, 114
trillium, green, 42
Trillium viridescens, 42
Triphora trianthophora, 51
trumpet creeper, xviii
twistflower, smooth, 81

verbena, sand, 181
Verbenaceae, 12
verbena family, 12
Verbena stricta, 183
vervain, hoary, 183
vervain, rose, 181
vervain, wooly, 183
vetch, hairy, 115
vetch, winter, 115
vetch, woollypod, 115
Vicia villosa, 115
Viola bicolor, 136
Violaceae, 8
Viola pedata, 137
Viola sororia, 138
violet, bird's-foot, 137
violet, butterfly, 138
violet, meadow, 138
violet, nodding green, 135
violet, star-, 196

violet, white dog's tooth, 38
violet family, 8

wallflower, plains, 78
wallflower, western, 78
water crowfoot, white, 67
waterleaf family, 11
water plantain family, 1
widow's cross, 85
winecups, 131
woodrush, 34
wood sorrel, violet, 120

wood sorrel, yellow, 119
wood sorrel family, 7

Xyridaceae, 2
Xyris torta, 29

yarrow, 202
yelloweyed grass, 29
yelloweyed grass family, 2

Zizia aurea, 159

Color Index

WHITE, CREAM, GREEN, BROWN, STRAW

acacia, prairie, 91: WHITE
anemone, Carolina, 63: WHITE, BLUE
anemone, prairie, 63: WHITE, BLUE
anemone, rue, 64: WHITE, ORCHID
antelopehorn, 167: GREEN
antelopehorn, green-flowered, 170: GREEN
arrowhead, broadleaf, 17: WHITE
avens, white, 87: WHITE
basket flower, American, 205: WHITE, PINK
bean, amberique, 112: PINK, WHITE
bean, wild, 112: PINK, WHITE
beardtongue, prairie, 190: WHITE, PINK, PURPLE, ORCHID
beeplant, Rocky Mountain, 82: WHITE, PINK, ORCHID
bladderpod, spreading, 80: WHITE, YELLOW
blazing-star, 140: WHITE
bloodroot, 71: WHITE
bluebells, prairie, 163: BLUE-VIOLET, WHITE
blue-star, fringed, 165: BLUE, WHITE
bluestem, big, 18: GREEN, STRAW, YELLOW
bluestem, little, 22: YELLOW, GREEN
bluet, prairie, 196: WHITE, PINK, BLUE
boneset, 210: WHITE
buckwheat, annual, 52: WHITE, PINK
bull-nettle, 127: WHITE
bulrush, great, 26: GREEN, BROWN
bulrush, hardstem, 26: GREEN, BROWN
bundleflower, Illinois, 92: WHITE
camass, eastern, 37: WHITE, BLUE-VIOLET

chickweed, clammy, 58: WHITE
chickweed, common, 61: WHITE
cloth-of-gold, 80: WHITE, YELLOW
clover, white, 114: WHITE
coneflower, pale, 207: PINK, WHITE
coneflower, purple, 207: PINK, PURPLE, YELLOW, GREEN
cranesbill, 118: WHITE, PINK
croton, wooly, 128: WHITE, GREEN
crow-poison, 41: WHITE, YELLOW
daisy, doze, 204: WHITE, LAVENDER
daisy, lazy, 204: WHITE, LAVENDER
dayflower, slender, 30: BLUE, WHITE
dewberry, southern, 90: WHITE
dock, pale, 54: GREEN
dock, tall, 54: GREEN
dogbane, prairie, 166: WHITE
dragon, green, 28: GREEN
dragonroot, 28: GREEN
Dutchman's breeches, 74: WHITE, PINK
elephant's foot, 208: WHITE, LAVENDER, BLUE
evening primrose, Engelmann's, 149: WHITE, PINK
evening primrose, large-flowered, 151: WHITE, PINK
evening primrose, Missouri, 151: WHITE, PINK
evening primrose, showy, 152: WHITE, PINK
evolvulus, Nuttall's, 172: ORCHID, BLUE, WHITE
firewheels, 211: RED, YELLOW, WHITE
fleabane, daisy, 209: WHITE
fogfruit, 182: PINK, WHITE
foxglove, false, 190: WHITE, PINK, PURPLE, ORCHID
frog fruit, 182: PINK, WHITE
garlic, false, 41: WHITE, YELLOW
garlic, wild, 35: WHITE, PINK
gaura, large-flowered, 150: WHITE, PINK
gaura, tall, 150: WHITE, PINK
gentian, prairie rose-, 164: WHITE, PINK
gentian, tulip, 163: BLUE-VIOLET, WHITE
grama, sideoats, 19: ORANGE, GREEN
grass, buffalo, 20: WHITE, PINK
ground nut, American, 99: WHITE, RED, PURPLE
hemlock, poison, 154: WHITE
hemlock, water, 154: WHITE
hemp, Indian, 166: WHITE
hogwort, 128: WHITE, GREEN
hyacinth, wild, 37: WHITE, BLUE-VIOLET
Indian blanket, 211: RED, YELLOW, WHITE
Indiangrass, 23: YELLOW, GREEN, STRAW

jewelweed, 81: WHITE, PINK, ORCHID, PURPLE
Johnny-jump-up, 136: WHITE, BLUE, VIOLET
ladies' tress, Great Plains, 50: WHITE, CREAM
lily, funnel, 36: BLUE, WHITE
lily, sand, 140: WHITE
lily, summer spider, 39: WHITE
lily, white trout, 38: WHITE
mallow, purple poppy, 131: PURPLE, MAGENTA, WHITE
marbleseed, 180: WHITE, GREEN
May-pop, 139: LAVENDER, PURPLE, BLUE, WHITE
meadow-pink, 164: WHITE, PINK
meadow rue, purple, 69: WHITE, PURPLE
milkvetch, Missouri, 100: PINK, WHITE, PURPLE, ORCHID
milkwort, white, 124: WHITE
milkwort, whorled, 124: WHITE
mountain mint, Virginia, 186: WHITE
noseburn, 130: GREEN
nutrush, fringed, 27: GREEN
onion, wild, 35: WHITE, PINK
orchid, three-birds, 51: WHITE
paintbrush, prairie, 193: PURPLE, GREEN, YELLOW, ORANGE
pansy, field, 136: WHITE, BLUE, VIOLET
passion flower, 139: LAVENDER, PURPLE, BLUE, WHITE
pennywort, whorled, 157: WHITE
penstemon, Oklahoma, 191: WHITE, YELLOW
penstemon, prairie, 190: WHITE, PINK, PURPLE, ORCHID
pincushion, Missouri, 142: YELLOW, GREEN
pink, mountain, 162: WHITE, PINK
pogonia, nodding, 51: WHITE
poppy, prickly, 70: WHITE
potato, duck, 17: WHITE
potato, wild sweet-, 174: WHITE, ROSE-PINK
pussytoes, 203: WHITE, PINK
rattlesnake master, 155, 156: PURPLE, WHITE, GREEN
redroot, 87: WHITE
rose, multiflora, 89: PINK, WHITE
rush, grassleaf, 33: BROWN, GREEN
sandparsley, Butler's, 153: WHITE
sandwort, Drummond's, 59: WHITE
sedge, hop, 24: GREEN, BROWN
sheep sour, 119: ORANGE, YELLOW, GREEN
shepherd's purse, 75: WHITE
shooting-star, 160: WHITE, ROSE-PINK
snakeroot, button, 156: WHITE, GREEN
snow-on-the-mountain, 129: WHITE, GREEN
spectacle-pod, 77: WHITE

spikerush, sand, 25: GREEN, BROWN
spring beauty, 56: PINK, WHITE
spurge, prostrate milk, 126: WHITE, PINK
spurge, spotted, 126: WHITE, PINK
stickleaf, 140, 141: WHITE, YELLOW
stonecrop, pink, 85: PINK, WHITE
strawberry, wild, 86: WHITE
switchgrass, 21: ORANGE, PINK, GREEN
ten-petal, 61: WHITE
thoroughwort, tall, 210: WHITE
toothcup, 76: WHITE, PINK
toothwort, 76: WHITE, PINK
trillium, green, 42: GREEN, PURPLE
twistflower, smooth, 81: WHITE, PINK, ORCHID, PURPLE
violet, bird's-foot, 137: WHITE, ORCHID, PURPLE, BLUE
violet, butterfly, 138: WHITE, ORCHID, VIOLET
violet, meadow, 138: WHITE, ORCHID, VIOLET
violet, nodding green, 135: GREEN, PINK, BROWN
violet, star-, 196: WHITE, PINK, BLUE
violet, white dog's tooth, 38: WHITE
water crowfoot, white, 67: WHITE
widow's cross, 85: PINK, WHITE
winecups, 131: PURPLE, MAGENTA, WHITE
woodrush, 34: BROWN, GREEN
wood sorrel, yellow, 119: ORANGE, YELLOW, GREEN
yarrow, 202: WHITE, PINK

RED, ORANGE, YELLOW

alexanders, golden, 159: YELLOW
betony, yellow, 194: YELLOW
bladderpod, 106: RED, ORANGE, YELLOW
bladderpod, spreading, 80: WHITE, YELLOW
bluestem, big, 18: GREEN, STRAW, YELLOW
bluestem, little, 22: YELLOW, GREEN
buttercup, early, 68: YELLOW
buttercup, prairie, 68: YELLOW
cardinal flower, 200: RED
chatterbox, 48: PURPLE, ORANGE
cinquefoil, old-field, 88: YELLOW
cloth-of-gold, 80: WHITE, YELLOW
clover, golden prairie, 103: YELLOW
clover, yellow sweet-, 109: YELLOW
columbine, red, 65: RED, PINK
columbine, wild, 65: RED, PINK
compass plant, 215: YELLOW
coneflower, purple, 207: PINK, PURPLE, YELLOW, GREEN

coreopsis, plains, 206: YELLOW
corydalis, golden, 72: YELLOW
corydalis, mealy, 73: YELLOW
crow-poison, 41: WHITE, YELLOW
cucumber, creeping, 199: YELLOW
cypress, standing, 175: RED
evening primrose, toothed, 148: YELLOW
fire-pink, 60: RED
firewheels, 211: RED, YELLOW, WHITE
five finger, 88: YELLOW
flax, grooved, 123: YELLOW
flax, prairie, 121, 122: YELLOW, BLUE
flax, stiffstem, 122: YELLOW
gaillardia, summer, 211: YELLOW
garlic, false, 41: WHITE, YELLOW
gerardia, yellow, 192: YELLOW
glade-cress, golden, 79: YELLOW
goat's beard, 216: YELLOW
goat's rue, 113: YELLOW, PINK, ORCHID
gourd, buffalo, 198: YELLOW
gourd, coyote, 198: YELLOW
grama, sideoats, 19: ORANGE, GREEN
ground cherry, clammy, 188: YELLOW
ground nut, American, 99: WHITE, RED, PURPLE
honeysuckle, red, 197: RED, YELLOW
honeysuckle, trumpet, 197: RED, YELLOW
husk-tomato, 188: YELLOW
Indian blanket, 211: RED, YELLOW, WHITE
Indiangrass, 23: YELLOW, GREEN, STRAW
indigo, western, 107: RED, PINK
indigo, yellow wild, 101: YELLOW
Klamath weed, 134: YELLOW
lady's slipper, yellow, 47: YELLOW
lotus, American, 62: YELLOW
lousewort, common, 194: YELLOW
mallow, scarlet globe, 132: RED, ORANGE
melilot, yellow, 109: YELLOW
melonette, 199: YELLOW
milkweed, butterfly, 169: RED, ORANGE, YELLOW
neptunia, 94: YELLOW
nits-and-lice, 133: YELLOW
orchid, yellow fringed, 49: ORANGE, YELLOW
paintbrush, prairie, 193: PURPLE, GREEN, YELLOW, ORANGE
paintbrush, red Indian, 193: RED, PINK
parsley, prairie, 158: YELLOW
parsnip, prairie, 158: YELLOW

pea, partridge, 96: YELLOW
pea, scarlet, 107: PINK, RED
penstemon, Oklahoma, 191: WHITE, YELLOW
pincushion, Missouri, 142: YELLOW, GREEN
pink, Indian, 161: YELLOW
prickly pear, 144: ORANGE, YELLOW
prickly pear, eastern, 145: YELLOW
puccoon, pretty, 179: YELLOW
puff, yellow, 94: YELLOW
ragwort, prairie, 213: YELLOW
railroad vine, 198: YELLOW
red fern, 194: YELLOW
rush-pea, James', 95: YELLOW
scrambled eggs, 72: YELLOW
senna, wild, 97: YELLOW
sheep sour, 119: ORANGE, YELLOW, GREEN
silktop, 103: YELLOW
stargrass, yellow, 40: YELLOW
stickleaf, 140, 141: WHITE, YELLOW
St. John's-wort, common, 134: YELLOW
stonecrop, yellow, 84: YELLOW
sundrops, 148: YELLOW
sunflower, Maximilian's, 212: YELLOW
switchgrass, 21: ORANGE, PINK, GREEN
tickseed, 206: YELLOW
tickseed, lance-leaf, 206: YELLOW
wallflower, plains, 78: YELLOW
wallflower, western, 78: YELLOW
wood sorrel, yellow, 119: ORANGE, YELLOW, GREEN
yelloweyed grass, 29: YELLOW

PINK, ORCHID, PURPLE, ROSE, MAGENTA, ROSE-PINK

anemone, rue, 64: WHITE, ORCHID
basket flower, American, 205: WHITE, PINK
bean, amberique, 112: PINK, WHITE
bean, wild, 112: PINK, WHITE
beardtongue, prairie, 190: WHITE, PINK, PURPLE, ORCHID
beebalm, lemon, 185: ORCHID
beeplant, Rocky Mountain, 82: WHITE, PINK, ORCHID
bluet, prairie, 196: WHITE, PINK, BLUE
briar, sensitive, 93: PINK
buckwheat, annual, 52: WHITE, PINK
catclaw, 93: PINK
chatterbox, 48: PURPLE, ORANGE
cholla, tree, 143: MAGENTA, PURPLE
cholla, walking stick, 143: MAGENTA, PURPLE

clammyweed, roughseed, 83: PINK, ROSE
clover, bush, 108: PURPLE, PINK
clover, purple prairie, 104: PURPLE, VIOLET
columbine, red, 65: RED, PINK
columbine, wild, 65: RED, PINK
coneflower, narrow-leaf, 207: PINK
coneflower, pale, 207: PINK, WHITE
coneflower, purple, 207: PINK, PURPLE, YELLOW, GREEN
cranesbill, 118: WHITE, PINK
crazyweed, 110: MAGENTA, PURPLE
dittany, 184: ORCHID, PINK
Dutchman's breeches, 74: WHITE, PINK
eryngo, Leavenworth's, 155: PURPLE
evening primrose, Engelmann's, 149: WHITE, PINK
evening primrose, large-flowered, 151: WHITE, PINK
evening primrose, Missouri, 151: WHITE, PINK
evening primrose, showy, 152: WHITE, PINK
evolvulus, Nuttall's, 172: ORCHID, BLUE, WHITE
filaria, 117: PURPLE, MAGENTA
flame flower, 57: PINK, ROSE
flower-of-an-hour, 57: PINK, ROSE
fogfruit, 182: PINK, WHITE
four o'clock, smooth, 55: PINK, ORCHID
foxglove, false, 190: WHITE, PINK, PURPLE, ORCHID
frog fruit, 182: PINK, WHITE
garlic, wild, 35: WHITE, PINK
gaura, large-flowered, 150: WHITE, PINK
gaura, tall, 150: WHITE, PINK
gentian, prairie rose-, 164: WHITE, PINK
goat's rue, 113: YELLOW, PINK, ORCHID
grass, buffalo, 20: WHITE, PINK
grass-pink, Oklahoma, 46: PINK, ORCHID
ground nut, American, 99: WHITE, RED, PURPLE
hyacinth, water, 32: BLUE, PURPLE
indigo, western, 107: RED, PINK
iris, prairie, 44: BLUE, ORCHID, LAVENDER
jewelweed, 81: WHITE, PINK, ORCHID, PURPLE
joe pye weed, sweetscented, 210: PINK
leadplant, 98: PURPLE
lespedeza, roundhead, 108: PURPLE, PINK
lily, celestial, 44: BLUE, ORCHID, LAVENDER
locoweed, purple, 110: MAGENTA, PURPLE
loosestrife, tall, 146: PINK, ORCHID
loosestrife, winged, 146: PINK, ORCHID
mallow, purple poppy, 131: PURPLE, MAGENTA, WHITE
May-pop, 139: LAVENDER, PURPLE, BLUE, WHITE

meadow-beauty, 147: PINK
meadow-pink, 164: WHITE, PINK
meadow rue, purple, 69: WHITE, PURPLE
milkvetch, Missouri, 100: PINK, WHITE, PURPLE, ORCHID
milkweed, swamp, 168: PINK
milkweed, twoflower, 171: PURPLE, VIOLET
milkwort, bitter, 125: PINK
milkwort, pink, 125: PINK
milkwort, slender, 125: PINK
monarda, lemon, 185: ORCHID
onion, wild, 35: WHITE, PINK
oregano, wild, 184: ORCHID, PINK
paintbrush, prairie, 193: PURPLE, GREEN, YELLOW, ORANGE
paintbrush, red Indian, 193: RED, PINK
palafox, sand, 214: PINK
passion flower, 139: LAVENDER, PURPLE, BLUE, WHITE
pea, butterfly, 102: ORCHID
pea, scarlet, 107: PINK, RED
penstemon, prairie, 190: WHITE, PINK, PURPLE, ORCHID
petunia, wild, 195: PURPLE, LAVENDER
phlox, blue, 176: BLUE, ORCHID
pickerelweed, 32: BLUE, PURPLE
pigeon's wings, 102: ORCHID
pink, mountain, 162: WHITE, PINK
pink, rock-, 57: PINK, ROSE
pinkweed, 53: PINK
potato, wild sweet-, 174: WHITE, ROSE-PINK
pussytoes, 203: WHITE, PINK
ratany, trailing, 116: MAGENTA
rattlesnake master, 155, 156: PURPLE, WHITE, GREEN
rose, multiflora, 89: PINK, WHITE
rose, pasture, 89: PINK, ROSE
scurf-pea, tallbread, 111: BLUE, PURPLE
shooting-star, 160: WHITE, ROSE-PINK
smartweed, Pennsylvania, 53: PINK
spring beauty, 56: PINK, WHITE
spurge, prostrate milk, 126: WHITE, PINK
spurge, spotted, 126: WHITE, PINK
stonecrop, pink, 85: PINK, WHITE
stork's bill, 117: PURPLE, MAGENTA
sweet William, 174: BLUE, ORCHID
switchgrass, 21: ORANGE, PINK, GREEN
tickclover, large-flowered, 105: PINK
tickclover, sticky, 105: PINK
toothcup, 76: WHITE, PINK
toothwort, 76: WHITE, PINK

trillium, green, 42: GREEN, PURPLE
twistflower, smooth, 81: WHITE, PINK, ORCHID, PURPLE
verbena, sand, 181: PINK, ORCHID
vervain, hoary, 183: BLUE, PURPLE
vervain, rose, 181: PINK, ORCHID
vervain, wooly, 183: BLUE, PURPLE
vetch, hairy, 115: PURPLE, BLUE
vetch, winter, 115: PURPLE, BLUE
vetch, woollypod, 115: PURPLE, BLUE
violet, bird's-foot, 137: WHITE, ORCHID, PURPLE, BLUE
violet, butterfly, 138: WHITE, ORCHID, VIOLET
violet, meadow, 138: WHITE, ORCHID, VIOLET
violet, nodding green, 135: GREEN, PINK, BROWN
violet, star-, 196: WHITE, PINK, BLUE
widow's cross, 85: PINK, WHITE
winecups, 131: PURPLE, MAGENTA, WHITE
wood sorrel, violet, 120: ORCHID, PURPLE
yarrow, 202: WHITE, PINK

BLUE, VIOLET, BLUE-VIOLET, LAVENDER

anemone, Carolina, 63: WHITE, BLUE
anemone, prairie, 63: WHITE, BLUE
blue bell, 66: BLUE-VIOLET
bluebells, prairie, 163: BLUE-VIOLET, WHITE
blue curls, hairy, 178: BLUE
blue-star, fringed, 165: BLUE, WHITE
bluet, prairie, 196: WHITE, PINK, BLUE
bog-iris, 43: BLUE, VIOLET
camass, eastern, 37: WHITE, BLUE-VIOLET
clematis, Pitcher's, 66: BLUE-VIOLET
clover, purple prairie, 104: PURPLE, VIOLET
daisy, doze, 204: WHITE, LAVENDER
daisy, lazy, 204: WHITE, LAVENDER
dayflower, slender, 30: BLUE, WHITE
elephant's foot, 208: WHITE, LAVENDER, BLUE
evolvulus, Nuttall's, 172: ORCHID, BLUE, WHITE
flag, southern blue, 43: BLUE, VIOLET
flax, blue, 121: BLUE
flax, prairie, 121, 122: YELLOW, BLUE
gentian, tulip, 163: BLUE-VIOLET, WHITE
grass, blue-eyed, 45: BLUE, VIOLET
hyacinth, water, 32: BLUE, PURPLE
hyacinth, wild, 37: WHITE, BLUE-VIOLET
indigo, southern, 101: BLUE
indigo, wild blue, 101: BLUE
iris, prairie, 44: BLUE, ORCHID, LAVENDER

Jacob's ladder, 177: BLUE
Johnny-jump-up, 136: WHITE, BLUE, VIOLET
leather flower, 66: BLUE-VIOLET
lily, celestial, 44: BLUE, ORCHID, LAVENDER
lily, funnel, 36: BLUE, WHITE
lobelia, great blue, 201: BLUE, VIOLET
May-pop, 139: LAVENDER, PURPLE, BLUE, WHITE
milkweed, twoflower, 171: PURPLE, VIOLET
morning glory, ivy-leaf, 173: BLUE, VIOLET
nightshade, silverleaf, 189: BLUE
pansy, field, 136: WHITE, BLUE, VIOLET
passion flower, 139: LAVENDER, PURPLE, BLUE, WHITE
petunia, wild, 195: PURPLE, LAVENDER
phlox, blue, 176: BLUE, ORCHID
pickerelweed, 32: BLUE, PURPLE
polemonium, creeping, 177: BLUE
sage, blue, 187: BLUE
sage, Pitcher's, 187: BLUE
scurf-pea, tallbread, 111: BLUE, PURPLE
spiderwort, Ohio, 31: BLUE
sweet William, 176: BLUE, ORCHID
vervain, hoary, 183: BLUE, PURPLE
vervain, wooly, 183: BLUE, PURPLE
vetch, hairy, 115: PURPLE, BLUE
vetch, winter, 115: PURPLE, BLUE
vetch, woollypod, 115: PURPLE, BLUE
violet, bird's-foot, 137: WHITE, ORCHID, PURPLE, BLUE
violet, butterfly, 138: WHITE, ORCHID, VIOLET
violet, meadow, 138: WHITE, ORCHID, VIOLET
violet, star-, 196: WHITE, PINK, BLUE